I'LL NEVER LEAVE YOU

VERNITA STEWARD

A wholly owned subsidiary of **TBN**

I Will Never Leave You

Trilogy Christian Publishers

A Wholly Owned Subsidiary of Trinity Broadcasting Network

2442 Michelle Drive

Tustin, CA 92780

Scripture quotations marked (kjv) taken from The Holy Bible, King James Version. Cambridge Edition: 1769.

For information, address Trilogy Christian Publishing

Rights Department, 2442 Michelle Drive, Tustin, CA 92780.

Trilogy Christian Publishing/ TBN and colophon are trademarks of Trinity Broadcasting Network.

For information about special discounts for bulk purchases, please contact Trilogy Christian Publishing.

Manufactured in the United States of America

10 9 8 7 6 5 4 3 2 1

Library of Congress Cataloging-in-Publication Data is available.

ISBN: 978-1-68556-973-0
ISBN: 978-1-68556-974-7

Today is a very special day for Chassaray, because she gets to see her boyfriend who loves her very much. Solomon has told Chassaray all about the ordeal, with Romona and how he fell for her quick scheme, so he apologized to her. Solomon has realized that he has probably met the girl of his dreams and doesn't want to lose her forever. So, now he has confessed.

INTRODUCTION

His name is Solomon, the man of many women, and her name is Chassaray. Solomon's eyes caught hers as they were both reaching for the stars. They aspired to being great, and so they did. They did it all for the glory of GOD. This book will convey things exactly the way, that things are today, as we go through our tribulations and trials. Neither one of them has realized, that their destiny is sure to be fulfilled. He's surely met the girl of his dreams, as they slowly find out, that they are soulmates. And though it seems that their destiny has been shaken, by many breakups and disagreements the only thing, that will hold it together will be the AGAPE LOVE of GOD. Chassaray, knows that it could end up being a tragedy, but it's a chance that she will have to take in order to see that changed man of GOD, she knows that he can become if she's the great example for him.

The Bible talks about whoremongers, and we all know that they're sinners who either were missing the agape LOVE at an early age and they now search for different types of LOVE to fulfill what's missing or unappreciated in them by the very men, who will suck their energy out like energy vampires.

Whoremongers destroy relationships, and will cause any one person in a relationship to exert twice the energy trying to keep up with or compete with anyone else, who may be interfering with the PATH of that relationship with negative energy. This negative energy that I refer to is the spirit of COVETING, which brings another spirit called jealousy and hate, which AGAIN will exert and dissolve marriages and relationships against GOD'S will. In this book, I simply describe to you the relationship of these two young people, who have fallen for one another. And with them in a similar fight against the ODDS of strong forces, who opposes PEACE period. Thus, the great SIN, but seemingly small problem can cause so much trouble if you aren't WILLING, as an adult man or woman of GOD to speak truth, which will always align with the word of GOD, and be our strong tower to help us stand, only if WE'RE WILLING! Willing to keep the peace even when we're courting/dating only. In the case of dating, the KEY to success is two honest spirits and like-minded people, who desire to keep their relations together, it will only be kept by GOD. This relationship between Solomon and Chassaray, where there are whoremongers trying to break it up on purpose, are simply JEALOUS and wishes that they could have him.

You'd think that his faithfulness would be easy, because she's very beautiful. Solomon, himself is a model, which means that he can have any woman he wants; he's always around a plethora of women, these females who would jump at the opportunity to be promiscuous with him no matter how dedicated he was, she doesn't worry through her trials and is confident that she can keep her relationship. She's a model and an actress as well, who's worked hard to get to where she is, and she deserves to have the man of her dreams in her life. Chassaray is determined with her gifts and anointing powers of GOD to kill the stigma, of the snatching of an unavailable man, although it happens all the time, and though it brings chaos in every way, she doesn't give up even when they try to intimidate her.

DISCUSSION

READ ON:

Scripture is **TESTEMENT**

1 KINGS 8:57 (KJV)

*The Lord Our GOD be with us, as he was with our
fathers; let him not leave us, nor forsake us:*

Before you read each chapter take a moment and realize,
that the characters in this book aren't real, our trials and
tribulations as Christians are, for they're a **TESTIMONY**
to the power of GOD, against demonic activity.

Believe on the testimony of CHRIST, that we may be
sealed. When we believe the resurrection of Christ in, as a
Christian, we're sealed once we confess unto our FAITH
to heaven according to our righteousness. At any given
moment of an attack of any kind in life; we must not forget
this important fact of our liberties and knowing who we
are. It is the subjection unto the honor of the LORD in
our heart, our great faith that is a direct connection for
protection on site of all trials. It is the **ANOINTING!**

HE WILL NEVER LEAVE US!

In the first half of the book, I wanted you to reflect on
your trials and tribulations and understand, that they're for
your assurance of GOD'S power as our source, through
testimony of the NEW LIFE given, unto us as believers.

It's very important we understand that, so that we don't give up as Christians in our long sufferings, after having confessed our beliefs, that He died and rose on the third day.

IMPORTANT

In the first half of the book, I want everyone to see, that we need and must not forget the **PRINCIPLES** of GOD, that we live by, as we allow the word of GOD to guide us through whatever pain we may face. The Christian body is made up of **members**, that we should be aligning with our **HOLY SPIRIT,** becoming better and more righteous every day. These members helps us to either grow closer to GOD, or further away from GOD.

There are **TWO** important members (body of Christ), that we must focus on during our trials and tribulations, to ensure we stay aligned. The important personal part of the imperfect vessel is: **"THE MIND"** It belongs to the Lord and should be put in submission to, so that all members are in synchronizing with the HOLY SPIRIT.

"THE MIND"

The mind is one of the most important members of our CHRISTIAN body, as it relies other parts to make one whole. The mind must be kept under submission at all times. And this is a process of killing the old man by will. Why must the mind stay in total submission? The simple answer is, so we can become more and more like CHRIST IN CHARACTER, and when we do, we shall not be lacking in any area, when it comes to our personal fruit for heaven's sake.

GALATIANS CHAPTER 5:22

The fruit of the spirit is **LOVE, JOY, PEACE, LONGSUFFERING. GENTLENESS, GOODNESS, FAITH, MEEKNESS, TEMPERANCE.**

When the mind is submitted to CHRIST His spirit overtakes the human soul and begins to infiltrate bit by bit "THE PURPOSE" He purposed in Himself, and that is so that we would become more and more like Him, and that His **GLORY** would be manifested.

NOTE: When it comes to the beginnings of our walk in Christ, it's according to the submission of our members. The important thing to remember is the SUBJECTION to the word of GOD, it must be planted in our hearts as a **PALM TREE.** We have to submit the members to His **"WILL"** and His word is His **"WILL"**.

REMEMBER: Subjection to the word brings character and character in practice is (submission).

GALATIANS CHAPTER 5:25

If we live in the spirit; let us also walk in the spirit.

When we're in the spirit we're more capable of being a positive influence upon the attacks of the enemy in every aspect of our lives. However, we can't keep the attacks from coming, but we can subdue them by staying in the spirit, and walking in it on purpose, by whence we do we gain power, through the anointing by obedience of staying in His will.

PROVERBS 17:1

Better is a dry morsel and quietness there with, than a house full of sacrifices with strife.

Never sacrifice your own will to take the plan to victory in area of life. When we sacrifice, we lose out plain and simple. Understand that on your job GOD is the way the truth and the life, by which my standard of living should supersede law, and this is where three important values/meet principles and produce manifestation. YOUR WILL(HEART), HIS WILL(WORD), FAITH(MIND).

READ ON: The "MIND" produces faith encounters.

In our mind we have what we call "FAITH ENCOUNTERS." Faith encounters in our mind represent the DICHOTOMY of thought and visions. These visions are GOD given and impressed, by the Holy Spirit into focus and once transformed into vision, they will be incubated in our soul for a lifetime as GOD'S plan. Yes, GOD will give us a mind to see Him for who He is in the spiritual realm, and eyes to see Him on the earth as He is in heaven and ears to hear Him for the measure of how far he wants this vision to go. Your frame of mind will determine your type of faith, be it stronghold or false faith. You will either have a faith that will align completely with your opinion or the word in GOD'S will, either way they shall both produce one good or bad. Again, this is why, it's always important to stay like-minded the Lord has deemed it necessary. Just as Christ loved the church, be it the same with us in every aspect of our being excluding the manifestation of who He is. Apart from these principles, we will only produce a false opinionated perception of His spirit amongst others, who know not the TRUTH. Which will produce a false faith=(equaling) zero manifestations and fruits, and that's what's important to GOD the production of fruit.

NOTE: **Manifest and always keep the mind of Christ. How do we manifest? Through total submission to His word, no matter what our trials are.**

READ ON: ISAISH 26:3

Thou shall keep him in perfect peace whose mind is stayed on thee: because he trusteth in thee.

I want you to understand here in these few chapters, it's very important to stop and think of how SYNONYMOUS, to steer and focus your "WILL" in an alignment with the word, because it will embrace your faith, because without the submission of the word first we can't form a relationship with Christ. It is your "WILL" synonymous to the manifestation i.e. the result of a future outlook totally dependent on GOD. Keeping our minds stayed on the commandments of Christ; we will never fall short of His character, and His anointed energy, which means GOD with us shall always abound mightily.

NOTE: The anointing, it is purposed for the glory to come at all times, though good and bad; especially the demonic forces that try and control us.

Jeremiah 17:9

The second important member to focus on is the HEART. The heart is deceitful above all things, and desperately wicked, who can know it? The heart is where the soul and is where the "WILL CULTIVATES" the desires of our heart. It's where the "WILL" to serve remains steadfast immovable abounding in the works; through the strength of what we "LOVE," it connects with the "MIND" and keeps us active doing the things of GOD. If we LOVE "Christ," it will not be hard to exhibit **agape** LOVE, because He will teach us His ways. As I have conveyed to you, that your **MIND**, must be in submission to the word, and so shall it be that when your heart is in the right place, especially in GOD, your character changes bit by bit. You build righteous character, by your will and heart being right with GOD, He then **IMPUTES** your righteousness. In your trials above all pain, never let the path change the focus and goal. The goal is to let Christ be seen.

THE HEART

The next MEMBER of our body, that we must keep aligned with the Lord, and is very vital to our growth is the "HEART." We must purposefully make sure Christ is lifted up in own hearts, by letting our light shine. In chapters 1-3, I wanted you to see the steadfast condition of the hearts of each individual. Some are already saved and are sealed with the Holy Spirit, by acknowledging Him, subjection to GOD'S word and will. Never let an unsettling spirit, which has come to vex you at the site of anger, be very quick to overcome evil with good. Difficult scenarios play out in our lives, which are seemingly out of our control, or at the very least gets us so angry, that we want to retaliate and hurt those who hurt us, it only creates more sin. The heart must be cultivated into the righteous growth, by which the good seeds sowed into the lives of others shall prosper better atmospheres in your city, within your family, and wherever we may reside. In these few chapters, I wanted you to see the hearts of the young people who are very different, some in Christ and some not yet, but how they were accepting to the seed sown at the very time needed in their situation, and GOD was able to come in and do a work in the HEART of people changing their lives and bringing people into salvation in Christ. Being honest with yourselves and GOD will manifest quicker wholeness in every aspect of our lives.

TRIED LOVE
THE STORY

Chassaray is a strong woman and guards her heart. She falls in love with Solomon, a gorgeous singer, actor, model, and businessman. He strings her along for a while knowing that there are many females who would love to jump into bed with him, these females could only hold one type of relationship with him, and it always means nothing. Huh, there was no real love from them, for they knew not true LOVE. Here in the city of Los Angeles, there seemed to be a stigma, a strong aura that stems from the heritage of the city's beliefs, and they all seem to live by it daily. Take what you want, whether it belongs to you or not is their way, but that is about to end, as GOD'S GREAT woman of GOD began to stand for what is righteous. And yes, that same stigma goes for relationships too. It's take what you want at all costs, even if it means killing and ruining other people's lives. Soon, GOD'S glory will come to stop all of the evil happenings with the AGAPE LOVE of Christ. For many years, the wrong type of LOVE has been a stronghold. Indeed, this is the type of love that has become as a tool for success and gain on every sinful level.

Love conquers all things they say, along with a little sex. Yes, the men in LA like what they call butter love—that's the so-called butter-colored skin females. The females here enjoy using sex as a weapon, thinking that it will blind and seduce every man they come in contact with, hoping that he will not notice how evil they are.

Turns out everyone would be wrong about Solomon though. He's young, strong, and intelligent, though he's also had his share of women, he deeply keeps Chassaray pinned to his heart as the one to marry. It's no secret of his many rendezvous, and he's not ashamed of his reputation. The relationship started out as being innocent: day to day small talk, until Chassaray gives into how cute Solomon is.

One day, he asked her to lunch. She said yes, and as they say, the rest is history. Solomon quickly realized how beautiful, pure, and genuine she was, so he asked her out again after the first date. Soon, they were a couple, meeting each other's parents and talking about their jobs, about their past and present accomplishments.

Her beautiful smile enticed him. He knew he had to see more of her. She had a million-dollar smile, one that lights up the streets of Hollywood. Her teeth were all straight and pearly white, and she had beautiful, creamy brown skin that had a radiant glow. She was Black and Asian, a mixed girl. Her mom was Jamaican and her dad was Asian and Black.

She had the typical skin color of an islander (Creamy Sun Gold) almost orange looking. Gorgeous!

Solomon is Cuban and Black, and he is gorgeous too. He stands six feet two inches with piercing black eyes. He has a strong and loud voice. Solomon's parents love Chassaray to death, unlike the other girls. They seemed to be and look like a perfect couple. Chassaray's dad doesn't like the fact that Chassaray has decided to see him more because he says, once a player always a player. Her mom likes the sweetness and gentle respect that he gives Chassaray, but she is no fool either. They first met on the elevator going to the second floor, and there are twenty-three floors in the building. This building happens to belong to the Moolunrig and Higgin's law firm, owned by Chassaray's and Cream's fathers. Mr. Moolunrig, Chassaray's dad, forbid her to see Solomon. The two would see each other passing on elevators, and she would give him a smile. This has never happened to him before. No girl has ever whipped him with a smile and her presence. There are lots of businesses in the building, but the law firm takes up at least four floors. The two law firms are different but are affiliated with one another by their corporate contributions to the same business, which thrives on the second floor for immigrants who need loans.

On another note, here's Chassaray, all day long she thinks of him, and all day long he thinks of her—about what a great time they have whenever they cross paths. One glorious Tuesday morning, as she was getting out of her car, she saw him, Mr. Gorgeous standing at his

Maserati SUV, and she decides to walk over and say hello. She says, "Hi, happy face!" Solomon smiles and says, "Happy face? What's the idea of calling me that?" "Well," Chassaray says, "everyone says that if you have a smile that could last through several conversations, then you obviously deserve to be called   HAPPY FACE, it's just like when people call me 'the girl, with the million-dollar smile.'" Chassaray is undeniably blinded, but she has yet to know the background and history of her lover's hands. They both like each other without a doubt. Sometimes when you really like someone, you suddenly get the eyes of a dove, seeing the way GOD would have us. He's a good one and they'll see it, as it turns out working here is about to have its greatest benefits for Him. Solomon works on the tenth floor as a stockbroker, and Chassaray works on the fourth floor for her father as a lead office accountant.

Since college, Chassaray has had a loving and nurturing best friend who has never left her side. Cream is her name and she's very intelligent as well. Cream loves Chassaray very much and is very loyal and committed to her safety as well. If Cream sees that a relationship or friendship isn't in Chassaray's best interest, she quickly speaks her opinion about it. She also doesn't really fight against the choices that she makes, but rather supports her. Cream is twenty-two years old. They both graduated from Harvard just as their dads did together as close friends. They get along fabulously. Their parents are both lawyers, as well as brokers, who make nothing less than two hundred thousand dollars a year. She is an independent woman, who also feels no need to run after a man. Even though Cream has heard of him, and she knows of his ways, and is very much against the developing romance deep down inside, but she will not allow anything that would disrupt the happiness of her friend. She loves her and protects her, as does Chassaray's father, who loves putting a smile on his daughter's face.

Cream has her reserved feelings and opinions about Solomon. Every day, Solomon tries to have a new surprise to get her attention, just to see her smile. He loves doing this. The thought of her friend being naïve hasn't crossed her mind, yet she's still one of the strongest women she loves and looks up to.

Friday evenings are the times the girls call 'me-time.' Their workday usually ends around 4:30 p.m. Cream calls up Chassaray and gives her the evening plans. Excited, she jumps and says, "Cream, tonight we're going out to have our nails and feet done, then mud bath at 6:00 p.m."

Every time they go to have their bodies covered in clay, the same females always ask about Solomon, as if she knew him really well. Chassaray never caught onto her until Cream saw the smile on her face as she rubs the clay on her face. Cream stares deeply and takes a deep breath.

Cream says, "This tea tree mask feels good already." Lying there, they finally close their eyes and go to sleep. Cream has decided that whatever Chassaray's decisions are in anything, she will stick by her. Chassaray is thinking of what a great life she and Solomon will have together.

21

Cream is very adamant and protective about Chassaray. She makes sure that every shortcoming is a staircase for her uplifting. Well, it's almost the weekend, it's party time at the Mexican club Drillos, and that means the chance for one of the whoremongers in the club to make a move as Solomon is out at Club Drillos on Thursday night. Cream and Chassaray are out at the church Bible study. He meets one named Romona, and she is a beautiful girl with long black hair, big breasts, a size twenty-four waist and thirty-six hips; she is Mexican. She sees Solomon from across the club and sends a note to him by the waitress. They sit and talk for a while, laugh and eat, and then he remembers he has to go and see Chassaray later, so he immediately jumps up and says, "Oh my God! Chassaray!" He tells Romona he has to go, and he'll call her again.

Romona asks, "Why are you leaving?"

He stumbles and motions to her, "I'll call."

Romona is a single mother of five kids whose mother died at the age of eight. She died of a heart attack associated with drug addictions. Romona would have to share shoes and clothes with her siblings and sometimes even dinner plates, and it took a toll on her because she became so hungry that she had begun to steal from the local corner store.

Romona would often remember the time when her mom's gambling almost got them taken away from her, and there were days when she and her sister would fight over whose day it was to wear the only pair of sneakers they owned for that day. Arguments had gotten so bad she ended up rebelling each time, and she would walk out to meet the nearest pimp for money. He treated her very nice, so nice it was unbelievable in the beginning. Although, she started out poor, she became a wealthy prostitute, and put all her kids through college.

Through the years Romona, bottled up so much hate for girls who were blessed with their mom, education and were naturally pretty. She had cousins who were very close to her, but they were gang and cult members who were savage at heart and would jump on a chance to ruin anyone's life suggested by Romona as a favor to keep control in society. It is known in society that this entity is the highest form of magic workers, and they will recruit anyone especially using young adult runaways and broken misfits. No one in society has ever challenged them, and all their evil deeds always went undealt with and left as mysteries. It was told throughout the community that the only way to have some sort of peace against their weapons were to use a crystal to block the negative energy. Today, Romona is recovering from a broken heart, and hopefully before it's too late she will get herself together in Christ Jesus one day. Friday comes, and she calls Solomon before 3:00 p.m. He's very uncomfortable since he's still at work and is meeting Chassaray for lunch. He puts Romona off quickly and heads to the fourth floor with flowers to Chassaray's office. Solomon knocks on the door, walks slowly over to her desk, and gives her the flowers. It's about 3:00 p.m., one hour before closing time. He smiles as she looks at him with a half smirk on her face and looking out of the corner of her eye. She can see the clock on top of the high-rise next door.

She asks, "What is this, Solomon? You brought me flowers yesterday."

He says, "Yes! And the day before that too. Would you care to make it a second lunch?"

She says, "Sure, I would. Are you gonna be coming to my place to pick me up, and at what time?"

Solomon said, "I will come by at about 6:00 p.m. tonight, is that okay?" "Yep, see ya then." On the way from his office, he gets a call from Romona to come and meet her at Starbucks for a cup of coffee down on La Brea. He says yes because he didn't want to make her feel bad again, being that he'd put her off earlier. He could hear it in her voice; it was shaky. So, he agrees to go have quick coffee. She only had on panties and a bra underneath the trench coat. He almost burned his mouth on the extra hot coffee he just brought. She smiles as she opens her trench coat seductively and very quickly, showing her thickness and cream-colored skin.

He's lured away by lust and takes another devilish invite and follows her into her home and stays for hours, having sex. He misses the 6:00 p.m. pickup for Chassaray. He's so outraged realizing that he's hours past the pickup time. How was he gonna explain it to Chassaray? It was supposed to be their first real date out. Romona was quick to impose first base and captivates his mind in seduction, now here they are FULL BLOWN SIN!! She didn't even give him a chance to suspect, that she was anything more than a lost promiscuous chick. Chassaray's at home, upset that he didn't have the decency to call. After cheating Solomon's embarrassed and almost afraid to call her, because he doesn't know what she'll say. HE MISSED HER PICKUP, as she was just about to start trusting him. He calls her around 10:00 p.m. and tries to tell her a lie about having car trouble. She's not falling for it and is really too upset to talk at the moment, so she says to him, "I've gotta go, I DON'T KNOW MAYBE, I'LL SEE YOU TOMORROW." "Maybe?" he says, "OMG, I'M SO SORRY CHASSARAY FOR NOT COMING!" "I'll see you tomorrow," says Chass (in her soft voice).

It makes him feel good that she says "I'll see you tomorrow."

The next day, he forgets the lie he told her about having car trouble and drives to work. Lunch time comes, and he texts Chassaray to see if they could have lunch downstairs in the café. This time, she's not so welcoming. She has become distant since she is the type that will not tolerate nonsense Solomon apologizes over the phone and pleads for her to forgive him. After hearing his voice, she gives in and forgives him.

So, later after work, Cream and Chassaray are in the mall, and they run into Romona at the cookie shop. They don't realize who each other are. The girls each order a half a dozen chocolate cookies, and Romona gives them a half a dozen of oatmeal raisin for free. They both smile at Romona and thank her. They leave to have a seat in the mall seating area and eat cookies. Soon, they see Solomon from a distance, who goes into the cookie shop. He reaches over to hug Romona at the counter. Chassaray sees firsthand who and what Solomon has really been up to. All the lies about having car trouble and the fact that she just accepts the apologies were too easy. Chassaray is speechless; the ill-begotten attitude of her boyfriend is surprising. She has lots of questions in her mind but would rather not even confront them at this time. She has a bigger and better plan. She'd rather allow the cunning and conniving attitude of the suspected green bow whoremonger be seen by her boyfriend himself, allowing him to forsake the ties of everything he's ever had with her. This way, Chassaray knows she has an easy win.

Cream knows how Solomon really is, she's heard it through the grapevine. Like many things that Chassaray is determined to do, Cream allows her to make her own decisions, especially with her man. Though she encourages her early on to let him go, the love for him has blinded her. Cream says to her, "Reality check, Chassaray, he's a player." Meanwhile, Cream is a head secretary and intern recruiter for her own dad's firm, which is affiliated with the Moolunrig firm, their fathers both went to college together and were great friends. Cream is very outgoing in their business too. She's quick on her feet and straight to the point. She's a perfectionist at everything. She smiles at every circumstance and never lets the world see her cry. She's adored by her father. She's top notch on her job, and she is up for her vacation. She's planning on going to the Bahamas where there are plenty of beautiful men there. Today is a new day for Chassaray, she's decided to venture out and see the world. She knows that her work takes precedence over everything, but she needs a break from people in general. She's decided that the only way to understand life for what it truly is and change it to start writing and journaling everything precisely in what she hears and sees around her. Chassaray has decided to take a couple weeks off just before Cream goes on her vacation. They're both going to a Caribbean Island—Chassaray, the Bahamas, and later, Cream to St. Croix. She likes to control everything in the way it should be.

So, she starts to write, and things began to happen, almost how she wanted them to. She's amazed and astonished. She needed this because there were some demonic forces trying to control her and her relationships. Whenever she gets like this, she feels that she can writing her troubles away or either reading them away, is how she found comfort in being frustrated. Chassaray went on an appointment for today, and she took the long route to beat all, but evil was ever so present, still trying to annoy her and her family and relationships. It soon stopped and the different types of gangs soon have no power over Los Angeles, as did no gangs in the US, because of the ripple effect of obedience to serve only Christ witnessed. They've screwed with her far too long on these buses and trains and in society period, totally forgetting who the GOD of heaven was, they had no respect.

Mr. Moolunrig nor Solomon knows nothing about the

creepy ordeals that Chassaray has been going through.

She's been keeping this from them, too afraid that they'd lash out to protect her and become victims too. Or think that she was crazy, when she tells them, that she thinks that it's a cult gang with wizards and witches, who works magic. It was just too much for her to bear getting others involved. After all, it seems they were only targeting her. The three gang members happen to be cousins of Romona. Chassaray doesn't know that they're Romona's cousins or she would've sworn that Romona set up all the attacks. It's Monday morning, they're back at work. Mr. Moolunrig has noticed that Solomon had been bringing flowers up to the fourth floor, and he wants to know what kind of relationship she has with him.

COMMITMENT TO HIS LIGHT & HIS WISDOM

So, he calls on the acknowledgments of his close friend and business partner, Mr. Higgins, Cream's father. Mr. Moolunrig loves his daughter and hates to see her hurt by other men. If he knew that Solomon was cheating and taking advantage of his daughter, he'd have someone rough up Solomon really quick. Chassaray sees the relationship as going nowhere fast and decided that she would tell Solomon just that the next time they are together. Solomon being the very determined, persistent, and sometimes very ruthless man, would never give in to Chassaray's decision to let things go just as he had in other relationships in the past. The secret of Solomon was that he'd been charged with assault and battery against his ex-girlfriend's lover who evidently broke them up. Cream knew about the little secret through a friend who worked at the police station, once informed about it she was forbidden not to say a word to protect Solomon's family name.

Chassaray has decided that just because it's so early in the relationship that maybe it wouldn't be a good idea to keep trying to impress her with the flowers after all she's has seen him with Romona on her job in the mall. Solomon was speechless and could say nothing. "But I guess, yes, it was me hugging her, but what makes you think that we're not just friends?

Chassaray says, "It's the kind of a kiss that you planted on her holding her chin." "Okay! So, the kiss wasn't so friendly, but I wanna get to know you, Chassaray. Please forgive me!" "Why should I?" says Chassaray. "Please, Chass." As he charms her with the lick of his

lips as she smiles. Chassaray looks at him with the look of unbelief and says to him, "Okay. You need Jesus! But you better not be watching any other chicks." "I'm not, I promise. It's you that I want. There's a movie makers festival in town that week." Since Chassaray and Solomon both does acting on the side, Chassaray has decided that she'd like to go, and Solomon asked if she'd like to come along with him.

"Yes! I'd love to go," the happy Chassaray says. She's excited about meeting many celebrities at the carnival. "What time? "We should get there rather early to find a place to park." Solomon will be meeting Chassaray at the train station, being that he's told her that he had car trouble just in case she'd ask. He's still being a liar. So, they meet up at the corner of Melrose St. and walked to the train station. "So," she asks, "Whatever happened to your car?" He says, "The tire blew out! Yeah, that's right, the tire blew out." Chassaray says. "Okay. How'd you get to work on Monday? My dad is getting suspicious about us and asking questions about the flowers you're giving me daily." "Why? I'm a cool guy." "My father usually is." So, they meet up at the corner of Melrose St. and walked to the train station. Chassaray, at the train station, being that he's told her that he had car trouble just in case, she asks, "My dad is asking questions about the flowers you've been bringing me." "Really? I saw him, and it seemed as though he wanted to ask me something. He walked by and paused and looked at me."

"My dad's very inquisitive about everyone that take a sudden interest in me. "Is that so?" says Solomon.

"Yes, Solomon. He likes to know their family history, and the number one question is, does he have a job?" Chassaray's persistence to keep showing Solomon her unconditional love goes on because she wants to see if he's the one for marriage. Later the next week, two girls one with brown hair, and the other with blond hair, both around five feet four, and one black and the other is Mexican. They split up, and the Mexican chick is headed to the park, nearby where Chassaray and Solomon are. She lies down on the ground unto her towel and stretches into a beautiful pose as if she was at work modeling, then she looks over at Solomon and smiles. She has beautiful gold skin, which made her skin look like a spray tan, and that much more beautiful. She soon gets up and walks over to the snow cone stand and gets a cone, then she goes and sits back down and turns to Solomon, while

Chassaray's head is turned, and she licks it very slowly and then Solomon's eyes grew bigger, and he starts to go into a trance almost staring back. Chassaray asks, "What is wrong?"

He says, "It's just so hot out here. Would you like a snow cone? "Yes." So, he goes and gets Chassaray a peach snow cone and some yellow roses. He looks and sees the girl that was lying on the ground getting up and putting her things away as if she were getting ready to leave. So were they. He keeps watching the female as it seems she is doing the same to him. Solomon and Chassaray are leaving for the train station, walking. They're walking and talking, and suddenly a voice says "Hi." out of nowhere. The girl has caught up to them walking and asks if they'd like to buy some necklace beads. She did it for conversation. She already knows they are a couple, but she doesn't care. The girl has introduced herself as being Abbey. They reach the train station, and she gives Solomon a business card. The card says, "the bead maker." Chassaray is not even suspicious of her tactic to get Solomon to call her. It doesn't even cross her mind, but she doesn't even know what kind of person Solomon really is. This man loves beautiful women.

The next day he picks up the card and decides to call it and Abbey answers the call. She's surprised and gets right to the point of what she really wanted with him. Abbey says, "I thought you were a very attractive." And she lies and says that she thought they were siblings, knowing that she saw them holding hands. This girl is desperate for

Solomon. "I've heard you were a very sweet guy. Could we go out on a secret date?" Solomon is dumb and says, "Yes." The date is arranged, and Solomon meets Abbey on Sunset Blvd. with her three cousins, which are gang members who want to learn more about Solomon for his riches. Solomon drives a light-blue Bugatti. She knows that her cousins will be assisting on this date, and it wouldn't be secret.

The explanation for them coming is that she has a curfew, and the guys have to come, which is a lie. Solomon asks few questions of them, but they ask many of him. Like where does he live and who are his parents. These Mexican gang members are used to robbing her secret dates, who are always rich and handsome, but this will be their last robbery, as they will get caught, and a Chassaray prays the word of GOD upon the situation. They take Solomon to a house party on Hollywood Blvd, where many famous celebs hang out to throw him off. They get him drunk, and Abbey sleeps with him. Afterward, they go down to the boardwalk of Hollywood and stop to a tattoo shop, and he gets a tattoo with her name. How stupid! He's never been this drunk before. At this point, he's loving all the fun they are having, until they almost drive to Vegas.

Later, Solomon and Abbey go to a hotel room and the guys drove them there and take Solomon's keys and go for a joy ride and get a ticket for speeding. Solomon wakes the next morning and looks for his car and it's gone. He wakes Abbey, a girl he doesn't know and also lies about having a curfew and stayed the night with him. She says,

"Maybe my cousins have it." Indeed, they had it and got it towed. Now he has to call his best friend Chassaray to get him out of this one by picking him up. She finds out all about his cheating when there's no one else to pick him up except her. He cries and pleads with her not to leave him and to help him get over the lustful stronghold, and she does, and he explains how everything had happened. Chassaray begins to cry while he's talking to her. He asked her not to cry because he was so sorry for hurting her, and he'd do anything to make it up to her, even if it meant giving his life to the Lord.

She stops crying, and she explained to him how the gang members had been taunting her for almost two years now, and that she believes that they're looking for something within her that she couldn't possibly give up to them. She tells him how they just sit and stare at her, or they'll come up to her and say things like "We want you and we'll do whatever it takes to get what we want." One week later, she's on the train to Universal Studios and there they are wearing black pants and black shirts. Members of the gang sent this girl to get close to Chassaray by having the girl hit on her boyfriend and steal him away. These gang members are mostly Mexicans. They're a cult who use devilish tactics to try and intercept or steal the blessings out of Chassaray's family, but she has declared and decreed that with the blood of Jesus, she was going to keep them out. She's encountered a lot of them since she's been out today. They've planted themselves in different places to try and hinder her blessings.

When they come, they use their own tactics of how to gain it, things and tricks from the underworld. She's blocking it with her faith in Jesus and the written Word. She's powerful, and they know it. She loves Jesus and hates sin and has a heavy **anointing** on her. She sits on the bus and notices them noticing her. They are studying her ways to see how she does things. They're always on her trail, noticing her every attempt to advance in the kingdom of God. She hates it, but she can do nothing but write them away and pray. It's more than therapy for her. Writing down her experiences at the time that they happen seem to change the present situation happening at that moment. It all seems like a magical dream, so she pretends to write them away. Knowing that these were some very **REAL** wicked cult gang members, she keeps her faith as her weapon anyway, she has to because she knows she has nothing else.

She pretends she has a magical pen that writes and puts things into place. It really works for her! Not realizing who they're messing with, they take chances. Today, there are three kinds of people on the train, and they think she doesn't even notice them. They're black, white, Mexicans with long and short hair and some with computers. They step off the train but realize that their life has now changed for trying to screw with Chassaray. Chassaray steps off the train and takes a walk to the grocery store and she finds out that they're waiting for her in Walmart strategically to follow her around in the store and use their tactics to hinder her. She doesn't even know how they know who she is or what she would look like, but they do. Cream thinks that this all started since Solomon entered Chassaray's life. Cream thinks that he is just bad luck for her.

Cream couldn't understand why Chassaray was the only one experiencing those episodes of torment. What Cream doesn't understand is that it is the gifts of God that are actually being targeted inside Chassaray. Since she can't understand or make sense of it, she blames Solomon for everything. Cream aches in pain watching Chassaray work so hard, yet not making any rational decision when it comes to her boyfriend, knowing that he is just poison to her. Chassaray has had only a few boyfriends in her life. All of those boyfriends have cheated her and not appreciated how beautiful she was. Though Chassaray was witty, sweet, smart, and innocent, she's always felt not good enough. It was just not enough to get her the man of her dreams, so she has held her own for years of tough times of being lonely. It hasn't been easy, but she knows that God is with her. Being the good girl is what mattered most to Chassaray. Chassaray's respect for herself and others has gained her the outspoken character that she has. Chassaray has impeccable and risky taste in men.

They've always been the men of higher statue, hunks, and handsome, intelligent, and rich too. Solomon's riches have brought him women on every end, but there's a twist to him: being so irresistible, he's also very manipulative and abusive to them all, mentally. Chassaray doesn't have a dark side, but she has a will to deal with people who mess with her. These men use cell phones to call up the demonic forces from hell, all to harm Chassaray and her relationship. They want to break her and her boyfriend up because they know that if they both get together, they will become very powerful. The more that they love each other, the stronger in God they become.

The gang members carry notebooks, basketballs, etc., trying to obtain things. It was their way of thinking and faith that had them carry different items around. Carrying them around her would enable them to become smart and greater than Jordan in basketball. Now, the pin drop has begun. Chassaray has called Solomon now to tell him about the different members of the gang stalking her; she tells him that she can see them. Solomon doesn't believe the fact that there are people following her, and she doesn't even know who they are or why. He's acting all nonchalant about the situation. She really gets annoyed at the fact that she's not taken seriously by anyone, even when she has talked to her mom and dad. It has finally taken a toll on Chassaray. It's Wednesday night. Hump night! A night that parties begin, and mouths and attitudes are popping, it's a time when everyone gets overly excited about the weekend coming up.

Cream is out looking for Chassaray, wondering where she could be, it was so usual for her not to have showed up, they've usually met up by now, and their usual girl time is between 3:00 and 5:30 p.m. Shopping sprees, salons, and so forth is their destiny for pretty girl Friday. It's around

7:30 p.m, and Cream hadn't heard from Chassaray. She decides to ride around, coasting in her black Mercedes Benz. Cream rode toward Solomon's house and doesn't see Chassaray car, so she becomes worried because it's not like Chassaray to miss calling or checking. She decides to ride to her family's cabin home and sees the Mercedes Benz. She gets out and rushes to the door and calls her name, "Chass! Chass! Chassaray! Where are you? It's me, Cream! What's happening? You haven't called or texted me all day! I'm worried about you, girl! Chass, we've missed our girls' day out!" She knocks again for the last time very loudly, then Chassaray slowly opens the door and gives her a smile.

Chassaray says, "Girl, I'm in the worst pain, and I've come here to clear my head of some things that were really beating at me. I know you think otherwise, but I could fix Solomon's hunger and thirst for other woman." She's not like the other women. She feels like she should be respected, and she demands it. She thinks that she's the one for him because she's a virgin and has God in her life. Solomon loves Chassaray, and he's playing musical chairs with women to buy time. So, he plays with her mind to make her want him more. Solomon is indeed a man who loves the attention of women—period. The fact that there are thousands of women who want to take her place, Chassaray doesn't waver with her faithfulness because now she knows that there will be people hating on the relationship just to be able to break it. She knows and feels the fact that there are people following her on trains and buses to try and find out things about her and what she's all about.

Some of these stalking people are the family members of the females who wants Solomon. Chassaray hates the fact that she can see these people following her, but she is helpless to the total dominant ignorance in the city. She knows that God's power is above all wickedness. One day, while going out for lunch, she realizes that maybe she is being a little bit too observant, seeing things that her mind is telling her instead of the fact that people are living and being themselves. So, she decides to stop thinking that way and live a normal life. The next day, Chassaray decides she wants to take more catwalk classes to become even better at her model walk.

So, in an effort to end her stay away trip to the cabin from everything and Solomon. Chassaray calls her best friend Cream to see if she wanted to go the theater for the catwalk classes. Cream says yes as long as it is after four o'clock. So, they're out. It's a Thursday, and Thursdays are the days were the girls usually go shopping for the weekend extravaganza. Their outings usually consist of trying on expensive jeans, Gucci shoes, and perfumes, which are breathtaking. Cream and Chassaray are usually excited about their girly day out. The two are always full of radiant smiles. They are small in frame and wear the baddest of clothes. The girls have a great time out at the catwalk class. Well, it's summertime and the skies are white with meshes of blue enhancing the bright sun that lurks behind. During the summer, there is a lot of beach partying, surfing, and swimming. So, the girls decided they needed new swimsuits for the summer. The beach brings about exciting chances to meet new people. The girls always meet new friends who would love to have their phone number. In the past, they never took any of the opportunities seriously. Cream now decides to make a change just to make new friends. This year, she's decided to invite some people who are compatible and fun to visit her. She wants to give them an opportunity that she didn't before.

Chassaray certainly felt a great sense of relaxation while sitting at the cabin home reminiscing about Solomon. If and when she thought of him, she wanted to think of the good things that could bring amends to their relationship. Meanwhile, back at the office, there's been a new addition to the board of directors to the accountant law firm. Chassaray realizes that if her dad is adding more to the team without her knowing or her presence, then it must have been important and urgent. She decided that before she goes back to work, she will decide to treat herself to a week-long vacation to the Bahamas really soon. He goes and tells her dad that she thinks she needs time off far away. Mr. Moolunrig agrees and says yes. He asks if Cream would be going, and she says no, that it was just a spur-of-the moment decision. She decided that she would be leaving at three o'clock on Friday morning, which is tomorrow. So, she calls Cream and tells her about the trip and asks if she would take her to the airport, and Cream says, "Of course."

It's two thirty and the plane leaves in thirty minutes and will arrive in the Bahamas at twelve noon on Friday. Chassaray didn't want to tell Solomon about her trip to the Bahamas; after all she was going away to try to get over her being hurt about him being such a Casanova. She arrives at 12:03 pm, and she goes to this huge, beautiful hotel. Surrounding her were lots of tourist. She even sees models walking around the hotel. She's happy she came. Chassaray is having a ball on her vacation. The only time she has thought of Solomon was once or twice. She's been working out and is getting to the top of her game.

ROCK LOVE
AGAPE LOVE WINS WITH POWER

Cream has been offered a second job and must decide whether to allow the responsibility of her first job to counteract the second. She's thinking that they should complement each other. Chassaray and her boyfriend have now decided to break it off for a while, least until he feels, or she can see that dedication and commitment. Neither one of them seems to be devastated by the split. He's still the number one player of all time. Chassaray and Solomon are worried as to who's gonna become each one's new lover. So, Solomon has finally decided to speak and say what he's been feeling about the grief he's caused Chassaray.

When two people love each other truly, communication is the main factor that help them take control of their own destiny. Just before leaving, Chassaray has demanded a better relationship, but also knows that a vacation away from him would help her see things in a better perspective. She's afraid after all that she'll lose him forever to the pits of hell. She loves him and will do anything to keep him, even if it means taking a break away from his presence. Chassaray realizes that forgiveness is the key to the whole relationship. Yes, communication itself destroyed their faith, but forgiveness brings it back even stronger. He's all she's ever dreamed of physically. She's back from her break that she took away from everything, and she sees Solomon out while driving her Mercedes with the top down just chilling.

Chassarasy stops the car, looks over, and calls him to her car. They talked a little while and then go for a walk in the park. He cries and says that he is sorry for all the pain that he has caused. So, Chassaray and Solomon are back together for a week and decided to allow some extra festive activities to bring them closer again. Solomon has a really close friend named Regan. He works for a marketing company and is very cheerful, happy, outgoing young man. Regan is a wild young man too. He loves partying and having fun on the weekend with his friends, smoking, drinking, and watching football. He's around the same age as the others, but a little older. Regan is always smiling. He moved here from England and didn't know he'd run into Solomon, who was very excited. Solomon's delighted because of all the stress of worrying about Chassaray's decision to leave for a couple days. Solomon thought about a double date and said, "Why not?"

So, he decides to tell Regan about his girlfriend's friend and then proceeds after that to tell Cream about Regan and to help him set up a date for the four of them. She says yes to the invitation and decided to wait until her outing in the evening with Chassaray. Each one is supposed to have on red and white, with a scarf and their frat caps on. Purple shirts and white jeans. The girls wear their outfits with stilettos. Their hair is down with curls. Everyone has on their frat jackets too. It's six o'clock in the evening and Chassaray takes Cream to Baskin Robins for some mint ice cream then tells her of this date being sat up for her and that she and

Solomon was coming along too. Cream says, "Okay."

"But how will Solomon find out?"

Then Cream says, "He already knows." Cream asked, "Where are we going?"

Cream said, "Out to the Ivy for dinner?"

"Yes!" Chassaray says, "The Ivy is a very expensive restaurant where only the elite gathers. Regan is very intense."

He's a weight trainer who's very tall, intelligent, and well-spoken. He seems to be really into Cream that night. After that date, they saw each other again. They met at the beach hotel lobby and exchanged numbers in passing. He has also played professional football before. Cream the experienced dancer and model. She has beautiful curves and absolutely adores Regan in ways he doesn't even suspect her too. She likes the fact that he's straight to the point and funny, although his ways of being loud and using curse words gets to her and is very disrespectful. She loves the fact that he wears a beard. On the other hand, Regan has an idea that Cream's feeling him, but she doesn't understand how deep the feelings are growing or how quickly. He's never been a relationship where he's expected to be loyal. He's definitely not used to being loyal, but he doesn't want to take advantage of a loving, honest girl.

Cream's a sweet girl who's looking for the heart of God in a man. She hasn't told her best friend about her thoughts, and everyone says that she is paranoid. Cream also is the type of girl who would never play around with love and take for granted how she feels for someone; she usually gets to the core of things about people and their feelings because her gifts are to be able to see through the hearts of people too. Cream is a kind of girl who doesn't run after any man, although she loves very hard. She has decided that the first time she encountered any cheating from him, she'd walk away feeling guilt free. Oh! She is indeed happy about the new love that has come into her life with joy. His smile lights up her entire day, especially when she's in a bad mood or when she's not so sure that she'll do great things at work like meet her quota for the day.

Cream's deciding today, she'll confess honestly to her father the reason she's asking for earlier departure time from work. She figures that leaving about two and a half hours earlier, she wouldn't get behind on her schedule of meeting Regan. Cream and Regan decides that they would like to hang out more, but Regan, has made up in his mind that he's not going to make it official, because he still thinks about his ex., but they hang out at the parking lot of Pet Control building next door, all day every day after work. One day he decided that he was done with the relationship, and suggested, that she be too. In the case of the other girls, he's never denied any of their affection and love toward him. They're always all over him. Oh! Cream hates the fact that her crush has a lil too much attention on him all the time. She tells her best friend about it, and everyone says that she is paranoid.

Mr. Moolunrig and Mr. Higgins are preparing for a multimedia meeting for their firms on November 27, 2011. This meeting will require quite a bit of the girls' time in the office so their fathers are about to start calling both of them in on a conference call so that they're always ahead of the game with marketing strategies to make their fathers' business look good.

They've done a great job all these years. The girls both receive rewards for great work. She knows that she has to prepare herself or her father will think that she's slacking and being nonchalant about the work. She thought, "I've loved this place for the six years that I've been here after graduating college. He really needs and depends on me. I'd hate for him to have to hire more help in the place of one or two of my responsibilities. It would just cost the company more money, and we're at our limit hiring new trainees. We can't afford the time and money for this when I can do it. I promised Father that I'd do all that I could. That way, he has less to worry about. Okay, I gotta run. I'll see you in an hour."

She walks in her father's office and rushes through to the back and drops her small thumb drive for the presentation near the garbage can in the front office, not realizing she has lost the most important part of her presentation, even though this is just a briefing of what her figures were. She took a chance, and it was the worst day she had ever performed for her dad. He was disappointed at her and so was she. She fumbled through fiscal year dividends from the West to the East Coast. Her sales were down, and she hadn't any proof to show it. Cream has left the office in a frenzy, and walking so fast, she walks right pass the janitor who has recovered her thumb drive. He feels that there is something wrong. So, Lopez, the janitor, has asked her what's wrong, and she replies with a cry. "It's gone," she cries.

"What's gone?" he says.

"My work of all the yearly dividends of documents I've figured up."

He says, "I never seen you in such a disarray and so confused."

It was a small object that contains valuable piece of information for quarterly balance for her team's effort in print marketing to show their expenditures. "Now, how are we gonna obtain ads to increase more customers?"

"OMG! Cream, I was cleaning across the hall in another office where I found this black piece, which matches your description, and I picked it up and took it to the lost-and found office."

"Okay, okay. Thank you, Lopez! I gotta get it." And she ran back to the office.

It's 5:45 p.m., a longer day than usual. She gets there and knocks, and a man opens the door. This man isn't looking for any lost-and-found items. He was there because he got confused as to where to leave his packages after hours. He'd just stepped into the room just before she busted into the room. "Hi, my name is Dicolda." "Hi! I'm Cream, and no, you shouldn't leave packages in the lost-and-found room."

"Ma'am, excuse me, but I must say that you are a beautiful lady," as he reaches out to shake her hand.

"Why, thank you," she says. "I really don't have time to talk, I'm in a rush."

"It's okay, ma'am. You look for whatever you're looking for. I'm here, I can help."

"It's a small, black thumb drive for my multimedia meeting today in less than two minutes." She says, "I got it!

It's exactly where Lopez put it."

Dicolda says, "I'll see you around again?"

She smiled and speeds out of the room thinking of Regan. "Have a great day, sir!"

He stands there, six-foot-three, and watches her speed out of the room. He was gorgeous, but he was never appealing to Cream, because her eyes are set for Regan. Regan's her gorgeous stud muffin. She goes back into the office.

Cream has been adamant about her work in the office; She's never let her father down. Although, she has tried once at the briefing, she has returned with the device to overcome a bad report, almost a minute late for her second half of the presentation, she storms in with all of her reports with a smile and her father is amazed.

"What's the smiling about?" he says.

"I'll get right to the point." As she explains the progress, she pulls out a thumb drive and shows the company's losses. He is intrigued with how she has kept up with her work, but he is distressed about her lateness. She smiles through it all. Determined to get the meeting over with swiftness, she says that though the company lost in sales, it didn't lose its revenue because of the ability to master mind a way of marketing. She recently has been thinking of taking a cut in her office time so that she may get to know her new friend, since staying at the office takes up the majority of her time and effort. I feel confident about the positivity he brings. She just wants to break the news to her father in a way that there is an understanding about the balance she seeks now for her life. She has never asked for such a thing, so it would definitely be a surprise to her father, maybe even heartbreaking in some small way. She figures she's only asking for her life to become a bit more balanced.

Although Cream feels obligated to her father's firm, she also knows that she has to venture out with this relationship because Regan is the guy she'd been waiting on to walk into her life. She needs someone like him to come and give her life, beyond what she'd already experienced. She'd been experiencing opportunities with guys who always took advantage of her caring and nurturing spirit. It made her feel that her self-worth wasn't good enough. All Cream wants is for a man to want her as their one and only girl. Cream has vowed to herself that she wouldn't let another man bring her down by letting go of her standards, so she kept her high standards for men, and now she has met a man who can fit right into her program of life period. They had the same major in college. They're excited by the same things. They are two ambitious people who want the best out of life. She wants to plan to go on trips and have many date nights with Regan.

Cream is so excited about having met Regan. Every now and then, she says to herself that it's too good to be true, and she smiles, and a tear rolls down her face. It's Thursday night, the day before she has to prep for small tasks of her father's multimedia meeting.

It's 8:00 a.m. on a Friday morning. Five days left before Christmas Eve, which by the way, was expected to be very cold. There's supposed to be around four inches of snow on the ground, a winter worse than last year with lots of ice blankets. Regan old friend, now an enemy to him, has come to town, and he's hanging around sightseeing and watching women. Jacob, a former army soldier, is a delusional and confused womanizer who has come to get his life together in this city, but he hasn't come along. He has come with a former soldier (Novis) who's wild and careless, and Jacob is the worst of them both. Novis is a gorgeous-faced ticking time bomb. These two have just rolled into town in a brown truck. Novis is a single guy who has a strong desire to be with someone but will not commit to them. In one week, the two have landed almost every club and bachelor party in the city, without a sign of ever slowing down. These two guys are a lot like Solomon. They are womanizers, when you live a life with three or more girls each day, there is no time for commitment. One day, Novis received a smile and a nice hand gesture from another beautiful lady in the gym. She surely momentarily admired Novis, who instantly came to a screeching halt when he met a young lady in the gym working hard on one of the machines, which happens to be Cream. He stops looking at the lady as he sees Cream. So, he walks over to her early Monday morning when she's alone. They both speak and introduce themselves. Things are seemingly okay for now. On Tuesday, Cream back at the office, smiling to see that Regan is smiling at her while looking at her with his arms opened and shaking his head.

He says, "My, my, my, lady of light. How gorgeous are you?"

She's flattered and walks very quickly into his arms. "Oh, Jacob, you're such a Casanova. How'd I know you'd say something like that."

"Give me some love, young lady."

So, they hugged, and he walked her into her office

door. Before he walks her into her door completely and let's go, he says, "You know, Cream, every time I see you, you make my heart fond for you. Cream, I really like you, and I would like it if we could go steady. You don't have to answer now, but think on it all day, sweetie."

Cream's at work half an hour later with a smile painted on her face and Regan's smile engraved in her heart. She's realizing that *Wow! I may have met the man of my dreams. Regan says he likes me, and I surely don't wanna let the opportunity pass. We're definitely compatible when it comes to ambition. He sure makes my heart warm. A girl has to feel that kind of thing from a man. Just to know that there's chemistry alone between us means a great deal. It means that there will be extraordinary activity going on—much excitement— and I'm in for the long haul. My father hasn't met Jacob yet, but it will happen soon. I'll make sure that Dad's happy with Regan. because he's definitely the man of my dreams. Thank you for sending him. Tonight's girls' night out. Instead of shopping, I think we should just go out for a glass of wine. Let me call Chass!*

So, she calls Chass at 11:00 a.m. just before lunch and tells her about the outing. Chass is excited about it and asks what she should wear, and Cream suggests that they wear fitted dresses and stilettos.

"What time are we leaving?"

"We're leaving at 7:00 a.m."

Chassaray says, "I'll drive my Mercedes."

So Chassaray and Cream gets out around 7:00 p.m., and they're riding around town looking for a great restaurant club type with great wine. They both choose the club Mazzio's. It used to be Solomon's favorite spot to hang out at, but it has been a long time since he has been there. Chassaray has really put her foot down and some of the things he used to do he doesn't do any more. He tries to respect her on every level since all his mistakes were pardoned. They both realize it might not be the best of scenery to partake, so they both decide to go to this little, small, neat restaurant club called Tao's, and they stay about five hours.

They both have about three drinks and neither are tipsy. Meanwhile they're having fun and, in this night, have run into Novis, the womanizer, who has spotted Chassaray and had taken an interest in her. He has asked for her number and if he could take her out. Later, they returned around 12:00 a.m. to find Regan's car sitting there in the driveway not empty, but idle with Regan sitting in it seemingly hysterical because he didn't know of the girls' night that was planned, and it kind of scared him. He thought something had happened to her, and it worried him crazy. Cream didn't turn her phone on since she was out enjoying time with her bestie Chassaray.

Cream's dad is very nosy when it comes to things about her. So, Mr. Higgins has decided to set up a date of his own—yes, a dinner date for his own daughter with another young man of his choice. He's doing this to find out who's the interested young man in Cream's life and if he is worthy of her. He has sought out a young handsome gentleman of his own to introduce to Cream, and he planned to bring them together through a corporate business dinner outing. Mr. Higgins had not mentioned the young man to . Cream yet, but he tells her he has a surprise business proposal for her, that would be a benefit for the both of them all the way around. He knows that would bring her new guy friend and that is when he will introduce the young lad he has found.

This young man has it all as well. He's a stallion and force to be reckoned with. He has planned to introduce this young man as his new hired employee. This young man is tall, six-foot-three, handsome, and very intelligent. He's an ex-ball player for the New Jersey Nets and is a very ambitious person. Men are naturally drawn to Cream and her beauty. Mr. Higgins knows that his daughter is a very attractive young lady.

Mr. Higgins sits in his office all day thinking of how the evening will go for his business that has produced a well- rounded daughter, whose life speaks through her profession. She is so adamant about her job, it makes easier for her peers around her to do their job. She also makes it exciting for everyone around her too. The office is filled with motivated, ambitious accountants, paralegals, law firm market, and stockbrokers.

Mr. Higgins has been a very wealthy man for a long time, running his marketing firm for more than fifteen years with great success. He has never taken a chance at losing his personal perspective of his company. Never had he thought of such until he imagined losing his daughter mentally on any level. So, he has thought of this plan to keep her interest within the company not knowing if it will work, but it's a chance to heaven he'll take. It would probably be a straight bore to her since this guy is strictly political conversation. Mr. Higgins is on the phone with Janie, the coordinator, arranging the dinner for tomorrow night, which is February 20, 2013. Meanwhile, Cream in the gym working on squats and lunges. She finds I'll never leave you just as appealing, funny, intelligent, handsome, and most of all physically fit. They both are. They're a lot alike. They both enjoy spending time together and are so excited with this newfound relationship. At work or wherever I'll never leave you is, he's always motivated although he's not in the same building as Cream. He thinks of their time in the gym, when he spots her or goes and runs beside her while she runs. They are determined to keep their spark flowing just as Solomon and Chassaray have. While in the gym working out, they both decide that before they leave that they'll go into the sauna and hot tub, so they go shower then go into the sauna and relax their muscles and share testimonies of how God brought them out of some detrimental situations and gave them a new beginning. Regan had shared how he'd been found with lots of drugs in his car, and the Lord showed favor to him and decided to let him out of jail the same night on bond, so he spent no time in actual jail. Earlier he had been diagnosed with a bad kneecap, which sat him out of ball playing forever, and that's when he started selling drugs.

THE DEVIL AND SATANIC PLOTS

Since he has been out on bond, he has been very attentive to make his life positive. He opened up a camp for young boys for basketball and teaches them the fundamentals of it and helps them build character by using some of their time to feed homeless groups, clean yards, and hold car washes to raise money for the camp. Cream surprisingly sympathizes with him about the situation with the drugs, and she doesn't freak out like he thought that she wouldCream is now thinking of ways now to break that news to her father because she's worried about acceptance from her father with Regan Mr. Higgins can be a hard one to deal with when it comes to accepting certain men as a companion for his daughter, even now that she's all grown up.Cream has never been one to sway away from the authority of her father; the men chosen for her has always been approved by him first.

The time has come, and they're in the hot tub; they've been there for an hour. Cream looks into his eyes in disbelief, but at the same time she's accepting of his past because she really has come to enjoy his personality.

Meanwhile, Chassaray is content with being back with her man Solomon, but she starts to realize that for him to be loyal to anyone is totally contingent with who he is. Chassaray realizes that she hasn't slept with him, yet he had admired her most even in all of his running around. Chassaray put her foot down and minimized the women that were chasing after him but that only worked for a little while, until one day, he finally got the nerves to ask her to sleep with him out of wedlock. This is kind of devastating to her because she doesn't know what to think about his sudden change in personality.

To sleep with Solomon would mean sin, and she wonders how she should approach the challenge of ever regaining her dignity and respect back. Sex is not important to her at this point in her life, but she wants to be in an extremely committed relationship with him by all means. Chassaray knows the benefit of reaping a bad reward just as much as a good one, so she has tried in the past not to overstep her boundaries as an innocent young lady. She confronts Solomon about his appetite for having sex, but what she doesn't realize is that while she was being her, which is hard all the time on Solomon, he'd actually gained respect for her being who she was. Solomon wasn't expecting to get to first base with her as he did the others in past relationships.

Usually, relationships with him wouldn't last much longer after getting to first base; things would begin to go sour. Somehow, after having reached that plateau in the relationship with others, he has thought of himself to be better than that particular girl. He'd look down on them for sure. Meanwhile, they see the Mexican gang members hanging out at the 7-11 store around ten o'clock at night. It was five of them wearing all black. Regan and Cream were out to just have ice cream and have fun that night, but they were about to come to witness a robbery that was about to take place.

Regan and Cream were cruising in his white Mercedes having a great time. At the store already was a beautiful girl who had just pulled up and was about to be robbed and harassed by two of the young men when they pulled up. The young lady, unknown to the gang members, gets out of her car she's caring a tan and white large Michael Kors purse carrying about fifty dollars cash on her. She walks over to the door to go into the store when the two men step in front of her and then one of them walks around to the back of her so she could not run back to the car. The young lady seems to be afraid, but not as afraid as they would like. They stand there in her face for at least ten minutes calling her, flattering her, and asking for her phone number, then when she says no, they become angry.

One of the young men says, "What do you have in that gigantic purse? What's your name anyway, girl?"

She says, "Move out of my way, idiots," and proceeds to walk around them into the store. They're persistent to irritate and annoy her by standing in her way to keep her out of the store while the other three are inside, trying to commence robbing the store.

Cream and Regan have just pulled up in their Mercedes looking great and very happy. They see the young lady trying to go around the guys and get into the store. Regan says to Cream, "I wonder what's going on here?"

Cream says, "Let's check it out."

They get out of their vehicle and ask the girl, "Are you okay?"

One of the guys says, "Is it your business, Mr. Pinky? They quickly shift from annoying the girl to making jokes about the pink tight shirt muscle shirt that Regan has on.

OMG! What was I thinking? Cream's saying to herself. *Okay, at least they're not focused on robbing her anymore,* she thinks to herself. Cream walks over to the young lady who's shaking, but she was fine, and Cream gives her a hug. She takes her to the car where she gives her a napkin to clean up her face because tears had formed up in her eyes from anger.

Cream asks, "Where do you live?"

"I live in the valley, Silicon Valley."

"Well, what in the world are you doing over on this side of the city? What's your name?"

"Well, my name is Shantell, and I was out looking for a spot for my spa sessions and saw this place next door. I pulled up next to the store to purchase a bottle of wine to drink to help me relax, and as soon as I got out of the car, they started to taunt me. I'm so glad you guys pulled up and stopped them from annoying me any longer. Who are you and where did your friend go?"

"Well, we're an honest couple, I guess sent here by fate to rescue you. My name is Cream, and the man inside purchasing some ice cream to bait the young men away from you is my boyfriend Regan, and he's not afraid."

Regan interrupts the gang's burglary by purchasing ice cream for him and Cream to take home. He starts to walk out of the store, and the three of the young men follow him out and one grabs him by the arm and says, "Aye, you don't mess with us locos here in east Los Angeles."

Regan says, "Get your hands off me." and punched him. The other guys came over they all started to fight with Regan, but then the cops drove up and they couldn't mess with any of them any longer. They feared the attention of the cops. Luckily, before they can get away, the cops sound the siren from the street. They'd seen Regan snatch away and punch the gang member. Regan, Cream, and Shantell quickly walk over to the cop's car and explain the drama and the cops asked the locos what were they doing hanging around the store. The two cops got the guys and asks them questions and then ran their info, and they were wanted for burglaries, auto thefts, and harassment. Regan and Cream had turned into heroes that night and were proud of themselves.

One of the gang members said to Regan, "We will see each other again, so watch your back, homie." The two send Shantell back to her side of town and then leave. They go home with their ice cream and have a wonderful night. Cream tells Regan how impressed with how brave he'd acted toward a group of gang members.

"I feel safe around you now more than ever, Regan."

He smiled and gave her a hug and said to her, "There isn't anything I wouldn't do for your love Cream."

Cream says, "We have to tell Chassaray, Solomon, and my dad what happened, then Dad will be proud of you for being so brave, and he'll change his mind about you."

Well, it's the end of the week now, and Regan is now happy and excited that Cream has decided to tell her father about their ordeal with the gang members at the store and how he protected a young lady and overall, saved all three of their lives and became a hero by going into the store, luring the gang members behind him into the store to taunt him instead. It's Friday evening, and Nicole has come to her father's office to let him know of what had happened a few days ago.

"Dad!" she says.

"Yes, Cream."

"Dad, I have something to tell you."

"What is it?"

"OMG! He was so amazing in the store being all cool, calm, and collected."

"Who?"

"Regan! He makes me feel free to conquer anything."

"What exactly happened?"

"Well, Dad. He protected us, her, umm, the girl at the store and almost fought one of the gang members who were trying to rob the young lady and the store."

"Well, Cream I'm very impressed with what the young lad has done indeed! What was his motivation to become so heroic at that time?" "Dad!" Cream says. "It was just his boldness and his love for me that pushed him to protect and be the man that I had always wanted around me. It was all quick thinking, pure intelligence, and love, nothing less than that. Please understand that Regan's love for me is real! He wants to prove his love for me, and I'm allowing him to be him and not fall victim to a worldly, fabricated expectation rather than just acting from an honest heart. Dad, will you give him a chance? I want us to have dinner together on Sunday.

Do you think that we can get together after church, Dad?"

"Yes, sweetheart. What time?"

"Four thirty will be fine, Dad."

"Thanks, Dad. Yes! Yes! Yes!"

Cream looks up and smiles as she thinks about Regan gorgeous smile. Regan has a smile that's brighter than a star on a Christmas tree. Cream calls it a million-dollar smile. *I better call Regan and tell him about Sunday's dinner that I planned. Oh, and I better call Chassaray and tell her the good news too. She will be so happy to know that my father is considering giving Regan a chance despite the plans he'd made earlier for me to meet the young man he'd chosen. My father obviously is willing to forget all about trying to get me to meet other men. Regan and I are going to follow our dreams of being together— period. He can be the gorgeous actor that he's wanted to be. Although he works at the firm and is very well demanded and respected very much. Regan has stressed that he's always wanted to hit the Broadway stage. I think that a break away from the scene of the office would be great for the both of us. We can at least start our dream careers of modeling and acting. We're both fit for it—in great shape and financially ready for the life of entertainment.*

Cream fears explaining to her father about wanting to possibly let entertainment be her first and major focus in life really soon. Cream plans to tell her father tonight after work in his office. She's been building up the courage all day, but she doesn't know exactly what she should say to her father. She's pondering whether to ask for time away or a replacement after she's found her place in the entertainment industry.

It's about three forty-five, almost the close of business time, and Cream headed up to her father's office to talk to him about what she wants. Cream walks up to the door and takes a deep breath, then opens the door. She says to her father, "Dad, I have something I need to talk to you about." Mr. Higgins says to her, "Cream, I hope this is some good news, I don't think I can take another hit today. "Another hit, Dad. What do you mean another hit?"

"What happened, Dad?" Now discouraged and shaken about the company, she now has second thoughts of telling him about her wanting to be replaced. "Well, Todd, my main chauffeur has quit. He's complained for two years about not being able to spend more time with his family, and I didn't give it to him. I was so busy. With my nose sea deep into our family business, how could I forget and become so selfish? He has a family too, Cream. OMG! Lord, forgive me. I didn't mean to make this man quit his job."

"Well, Dad, don't beat yourself up too bad. I'm sure if you called him and tried to talk to him again and apologize, he would accept your apology and would come back."

"I really don't think that apologizing will change his mind about how he feels right now. I've treated him and his family badly, Cream. I'm going to try and talk to him on tomorrow and offer him his job back with benefits. Maybe he needs a vacation, a spa or something."

"Okay, Dad, I have to tell you something now, Daddy. This is gonna be hard and unexpected, but, Dad, I wanna leave the company to pursue my dreams of acting. "OMG! Cream, what am I supposed to do without you?" "Dad, I figure you would have a good solution for the problem, without there being a break in the system that we've been running. We've an excess number of secretaries here in the office, and I just thought that we could afford to cross train one of them if it's okay with you. "Well, Cream, I don't think that it would be too much of a problem for us to do. Cream, would you do me a favor and let's hold off this conversation until after lunch. I shall have an answer for you as to what I want to do then." "Okay, Dad, see you soon." Cream leaves and goes on her hour and half lunch. She goes to her office to get her purse and her office phone rings. She picks up, and it's Chassaray calling from her office desk.

"Oh, Cream! Great you answered. Why haven't you been answering your cell? I've been calling you for about half an hour to tell you about the huge single womens' love conference that they're having at the Staples Center, which is starting at 7:00 p.m. tonight for three nights. Do you think that you would like to go and see if it would help us love our boyfriends a little better?"

Cream says, "Well, I think that it would be a great idea. I just have to meet with Regan after work and talk to him about what happened with my dad today. I told Regan that I'd tell my dad about the robbery that happened a few nights ago."

"Oh, yes! How did that go?"

"Yes, girl, I was going to call you and tell you about it, but we ended up spending more time in the office talking than I had planned, but I'm glad that you called because I believe that the women's conference would be a great inspiration to the both of us. You, Chassaray, really need to take heed to whatever information that inspires you to do better."

"Yeah, I know it has not been the best of times dealing with Solomon's wandering eyes of unloyalty. I have come to realize that Solomon's indeed a very handsome man, and I should welcome any compliments that a woman should bring, but at the same time, I have to stick to my expectations and morals. After all, it teaches him how to treat me as the great quality women that I am."

"Exactly, and although Regan and I aren't having any trouble right now, it's not to say that we won't have any later. I'm really looking forward to the uplifting. Great," says Cream.

"Okay, shall we invite Regan and Solomon to come along, or do you think that would be asking for too much."

"Yes, I do think we'd better go alone at this point. It's going to be an exciting night. It's girl time!"

"Chassaray, we should be leaving around six fifteen tonight, okay?"

So, Cream hangs up the phone with Chassaray and leaves the office to have quick lunch at the sandwich shop on the first floor. It's now one ten in the afternoon, and lunch lasts an hour, so she only grabs a sandwich before she needs to get back to her dad's office. Cream, at this point, is feeling rather anxious about what her father is going to say about her wanting to move to New York to pursue her dreams. She orders a turkey Swiss sandwich and sits down to eat. While moving very swiftly, she finds herself taking huge bites—it was almost as if she was in a contest to finish. She slows down a bit and realizes that she's making a big scene, only to look up and see Regan standing in line to order a sandwich, but he's smiling at her. So, she stops chewing and stares right into his eyes and covers her mouth with a napkin; she sighs "OMG!"

then continues to chew her food and then motions for him to come over.

He hurries over with a huge smile on his face and says, "My, my, what a Kodak moment." With a smile he says, "Might I ask where's the fire and why wasn't I invited?"

Laughingly he says, "It's just love, my dear."

She says, "Well, I'm in a rush to get back to Dad's office to discuss my plans of me moving to New York."

"Oh! Okay. Are we still gonna meet right after work?"

"Yes, sweetie! Just meet me right here at the sandwich shop at four thirty pronto! I've to fill you in on the discussion Dad and I are about to have. Also, Chassaray and I are going to a women's conference tonight, so I really need to be brief."

Regan kisses her on the cheek and goes back to get into line. Cream is always so happy to see her boyfriend. With a smile on her face, she hurries to finish her Turkey Swiss sandwich and moves right along up to her fathers' office. She opens the door and says, "Dad, I'm here." "Hi, sweetie," he says.

"So, what's your verdict, Father?"

"Well, I've decided that I'm going to support your decision. You've been here with me for some years now, and you've never complained about the company, instead you were always an asset to the company's growth. Now, sweetheart, I know that you've enjoyed your time here with great appreciation, so it's gives me great pleasure to support the potential growth that you so desire in ever so wonderful manner as a father. I realize that has God has truly blessed this company as well as this family, and I want the love to continue to grow full circle. Sweetheart, I love you with all my heart, and I want you to know that I've appreciated every day that you've come into work early just to make sure that everything was set up before the day began. You've stayed late nights to make sure future workloads would make the quota daily. Cream, I know that you're going to excel being an actress in New York. Cream, I do want to ask that you remember Sunday's dinner at 4:30 p.m. so that we may discuss this with your mom, who doesn't know about this yet."

"Okay, Dad. Well, I've gotta run now and get back to my desk and finish up the last line of progress reports according to the company's stock. Dad, I want to thank you once again for standing by my side." "You're welcome, Cream. Your mother and I will see you at Sunday's dinner." Cream takes off and heads down to the café so that she can meet Regan before she heads home to get ready for the conference. Cream sits down and waits for Regan to get there. She's super excited about letting him know about the response that her dad has had with both conversations. Thinking that it would just break his heart, she was really stunned with the attitude of him being invitingly excited for her decisions.

This has really been a great week for Cream. She's been showered by love from her boyfriend, friends, and family and her confidence is over the top. It's now 4:15 p.m., and Regan has showed up early as always when it comes to Cream. He always shows dedication toward her. Regan sits there for about five minutes tapping his fingers on the table with his legs crossed. He begins to sing the song in whisper "Forever Love," as he turns his head from side to side with a groove while he's singing and thinking of Cream with his eyes closed. He then looks up and opens his eyes to see her standing there. He's startled into a happier mood and there it is—that million-dollar smile that she loves to see. She smiles with her arms open and says, "Let's go higher, and they began to sway back and forth for about five minutes, and she squeezes into him and says guess what? My dad's given me approval of going to New York and pursuing my dreams!" as she screams out loud. "Isn't that great, Regan?"

"Yes, sweetheart. It's awesome."

"Also, there's gonna be a dinner on Sunday, and you're invited."

He looks stunned and says, "I didn't think that your dad approved of me!"

"Well, he's changed his mind and is now invitingly happy to have you there. Okay?"

"Well, it's like we're gonna start off on a good note after all, huh, sweetheart?"

She nods her head yes. "Regan, tonight, Chassaray and I are going to this women's conference tonight, and I'm leaving here very shortly so I'll call you tonight if it's not too late."

"Okay."

He gives her a kiss on the forehead, and they depart. Cream immediately calls Chassaray on her phone and tells her she's gonna run home and grab a quick shower and get dressed. Cream only lives five blocks away from the office. Regan is heading to the gym right away after work; it's his daily routine of sustaining a great boost of energy. He runs into Jacob and Novis at the barber shop across the street who are supposed to be his buddies. They've been busy trying to find themselves a little honey to date since they've just moved into town. Regan speaks to them and asks them if they would like to go for a workout session and then hangout at his man cave. Novis and Jacob both agreed to meeting up at Regan tonight around 7:00 p.m. for a good time. Jacob begins to tell Regan about the pretty young lady that he has met at the fitness spa.

"Regan, she is gorgeous. She has long slim legs, a small waist, very thick in the hips, and oh, her name is Simone and her face and smile is very graceful. Hey, she says that she has a friend named Sommers that may even be interested in Novis too."

"Oh, my God! I can't wait to meet these two females," says Regan. "Because you guys are the loosest scrubs I know, dude. Exactly what type of ladies are these, and where are they from?"

"Well, here's the spill Regan," said Jacob. "I was in the gym one day, and I'd had a pretty long hard work out when I suddenly became very dizzy and tired. So, some of the staff at the gym recommended me to go to the spa and lay down there, maybe have a quick massage while

I'm at it. So, I did, and it was wonderful. I stayed there that day for around four hours, relaxing, trying to regain strength back, but anyway, as I lay there and with my face and eyes covered with cold cucumbers and mango-berry mask, I heard a loud, obnoxious voice talking on a cell phone coming near the door with an attempt to come in. So, she opened the door. I heard her lie down next to me and began speaking with the masseuse next to me about acupuncture while she lies. Soon, her phone rings again, and as she's talking to her friend. I listen, and her name was Sommers. She wanted to go to the temple to see if they'd opened up a room at the temple shelter for her and her three boys there.

So, Simone said to her that she'd be there as soon as she could. She couldn't help but ask what the reason was that young lady had nowhere to stay, and Simone started to explain to her how this young lady had reaped the worse of karma, because she was a witch.

She had been mad at God for taking her mother and for so many years had been promiscuous with other women's boyfriends and husbands. She had been into prostitution, stripping, and even helped one of her boyfriends to distribute drugs and kill people and extortion for money. She had made him fall in love with her by using all kinds of evil and ungodly deeds. After summoning him to her, she then turned him from his true love, a very intelligent loving young lady named Essence, who was a real leader for God, a singer, and an actress, entrepreneur, and on top of it, gorgeous and rich. She truly loved him for him and just wanted to see him turn to Jesus.

"Sommers had become very insanely jealous of the young lady and tried to take her down by plotting to destroy her with the help of Zarcus himself, a very powerful man whom she wanted bad, but Essence loved. Sommers somehow contacted Zarcus, and they would meet at hotels for meetings and have sex. Simone says that Sommers was very money hungry, conniving, and deceitful. I was stunned by the story of the young lady and instantly knew that she was greatly possessed by the devil and in the dark. After learning how disturbed the young lady was, I was reluctant to even want my friend Novis to meet her, but I knew that this was a moment of personal discretion, so I chose to stay quiet for the moment, and who knows, when Novis meets Sommers, it just may happen that he's not interested.

"After that conversation, I asked Simone how long she had known Sommers and if she was on drugs. Simone says, 'I've known Sommers for fifteen years, and she's set in her ways, and for ten of those years, she has secretly been on drugs of all kinds, including her favorite, marijuana.'"

"I knew at that moment, if she was still on drugs, I definitely had to tell Oso before he meets her, because he's wild and everything, and even went as far as smoking marijuana, but those heavy drugs would definitely take him for a roller coaster ride. He's a wild party animal, but he's no crack head like Zarcus and Sommers. I lay there thinking how much my friends meant to me and how much I'd been wanting to change from being a wild man and maybe find someone to settle down with, but not with just anyone. I've always showed Novis love as a brother, the same love Jesus would show him throughout our years of knowing one another before and after the military. Though, we've failed regarding our relationships, I'd never let him fall into a deeper pit. We've got to find Jesus fast."

He peeled the two cucumbers off and then looked over to her and asked, "When are you going to be introducing her to Novis?"

She then said, "Tomorrow. I'm bringing her to the gym tomorrow, and then after, we'll be back here for the spa. I figured that Jacob could bring Novis to the gym then I could introduce Novis to Sommers then." "Okay, cool, because I'd like to be there as well. But first, I'm going to have a serious talk with Oso about this. I have to because of the drugs."

Simone says, "I can understand where you're coming from."

"Simone, thank you so much for sharing this information with me. You know, Simone, God is good, and in this situation, we've all the light we need to help two desperate people who just needs a lot of love and direction. Jesus is the answer! We all really need to find a church home and a pastor that's after God's own heart to pray for our sins. So anyway, I told her I had to get going and that I'd see her tomorrow, but the next day, Sommers had an emergency her sugar had skyrocketed, and she went into a coma, and so, Novis hasn't been able to meet her yet. The girl is in very bad shape, not to mention that she was on drugs while being sick with her diabetes."

"Regan, I'm really wondering who this young lady is after hearing this. I've never seen such a person so evil and determined to bring down the next person just for their own advances and everything all while being so sick. Wow! That's some kind of evil! I also wonder if she'd used protection with all of these men she was sneaking and sleeping with. Sommers could be passing AIDS or any kinds of diseases around. This story really makes me want to settle down, Novis. There's nothing out here for us, I think we'd be better off trying to find a mate through a Christian website."

"Well, how about we find a site tonight when you guys come over?"

"I love you, guys, and you've been my friends for a long time, and going the Christian route couldn't be better." "Aight, man! We'll see you tonight."

"Bet! Oh, Jacob, make sure you guys are sober tonight when you come over, okay?"

Jacob says, "Cool." He hurries to his car gets in and speeds off. Well, it's 5:00 p.m. now, so Jacob called Novis on his cell phone and tells him that he'll be over to pick him up at 6:30 p.m. to meet and go over to Regan's house.

"Novis, tonight is going to be epic, my friend! We're getting fired up and friendly with some really hot chicks tonight!"

Novus sais, "What? Just where are we going to be

meeting these young ladies, and who are they?"

"Well, Regan and I were just talking about this girl, Sommers, who Simone was supposed to be bringing to the gym, but she wasn't able to show up because she fell into a coma, and no one has heard of her condition just yet. The fact is that she's a diabetic, and on drugs at the same time was the issue."

"OMG! Really, Jacob?"

"Yes, and I wouldn't want my boys to end up with females who are promiscuous, unbalanced, and wild. In this case, this girl's secret issues could've very well end up being a disaster for Novis's life or anyone's life. I'm just glad we were able to witness her health issues from a far. So, bro, I'll see you at six thirty, aight?"

"Yeah, bro, see ya in a lil bit."

On another note, at 6:20 p.m. CREAM has arrived at Chassaray's for their night out at the women's conference. Chassaray's dressed in a royal blue, knee-high Versace dress with some blue Versace stilettos. Her black-auburn-brown streaked hair is pulled back into a crown with flowing curls on the sides and down the back. CREAM is wearing a long pink Gucci dress with white shoes and white pearls. Her hair is pulled back into a single bun. She's looking as gorgeous as a porcelain doll. Her skin is flawless with only a hint of Mac makeup on. They're as radiant as a light from a stage.

Cream says, "We have to get going! It's 6:40 p.m. I want to make sure that we get front row seats near the prophetess and bishops anointing tonight, that's were all of the fire will come from for healings. Okay, let's get going! It should only take us ten minutes to get there, otherwise with traffic it should take twenty minutes. I'm so excited about the spiritual restoration that has come our way. Lord knows that I surely appreciate the relationship that Regan and I have. We're both dedicated and committed to what's right for the sake of ourselves, our families, and humanities. I'm blessed to have him in my life, so I guess I'm trying to say that even though we've dated for such a short time, I actually feel like I've known him for years."

Chassaray and Cream arrive at the Foursquare Galaxy arena on Eighth Street for the conference at 6:55 p.m. Chassaray's driving her black Mercedes SUV. The first speaker for the conference was going to be a bishop from Washington State named Bishop Dahnogfet, a French pastor originally from Paris, France. CREAM says, "Let's head to the front."

So, they head to the front and find two seats on the front row. The conference starts right on time at 7:00 p.m. Worship begins, and the anointing is starting to flow as the Sunshine All time Praise team has begun singing, "Lord You Are Everything." The girls are instantly inspired to worship, ushering in the spirit of the Living God. Chassaray is worshiping and suddenly looks over past Cream and sees a woman crying out to the Lord on her knees, as she, too, worshiped from the spirit in truth. She's mesmerized of how intense this lady seemed to have been in her worship. Many thoughts were racing through her mind. Her first thought to herself of the lady was whether the lady was reaching Jesus at that very moment. Next, how long does it take until the Holy Spirit arrives.

Chassaray says to herself, *My God I can feel the power in the atmosphere so strongly.* So, she walks a little closer to the lady who's in deep spirits of worship. Chassaray kneels down next to her as they're still playing the music. Nervously, she asks the prayer warrior standing near her, "Is it possible that I may receive at this very moment what she has that takes her so deeply into worship?"

Chassaray, standing there in pure innocence and great zeal for God, wants to become closer to God for she is indeed hungry for his presence in a way she has never experience before. The ushers start to explain to Chassaray that she could indeed receive the Holy Spirit right now if she'd believed in Jesus Christ as savior, then she could surely get down into praise and worship as the spirit brings utterance of his language. So, she says to the prayer warrior, "Yes, I've accepted him as Lord and savior, but I haven't experienced the Holy Ghost and I'd love to receive it right now. She lay hands on Chassaray's belly and then her forehead that she would receive that Holy Spirit, and she did.

Chassaray begins to shake and utter in tongues, of different languages. She cries uncontrollably and begins to fall back into the holy presence of God for the duration of the worship. Meanwhile, Cream is at her seat praising and worshiping, not knowing that Chassaray has been caught up in the spirit. Cream, standing with praise upon her lips singing, she begins to open up her eyes and looks over to where Chassaray is. She's overexcited with joy to see what was going with her friend Chassaray. Cream stood there for almost a minute, then she started, in hesitation, toward her. She looked at the interceder, and she asked her if she has the Holy Ghost, and she smiled at her and nodded her head. "Yes, my sister." Cream says, "Well I'd like to receive the Holy Ghost too! Will it be hard to receive?" The prayer warrior said to her, "No, it's not hard to receive." The interceder picks up a bottle of oil from the altar holding out her hand. She says to Cream, "Come here." She first asks if she's received Jesus as her Lord and savior.

Cream replied to her, "Yes," then she touches the young lady's forehead while at the same time touching her stomach and speaking into tongues. Suddenly, Cream begins to speak in tongues too. Cream shouts out, "Thank you, Jesus!"

It's been thirty minutes into worship, and service is about to start. Chassaray has gotten up, and she walks over to the altar and finds her bestie Cream standing there with tears in her eyes. Chassaray grabs her hand and says, "Cream, I love you." and Cream says, "I love you too."

They walk back to their seats holding hands, smiling with the joy of the Lord in their hearts. Chassaray tells Cream that she's had the best thing ever to happen to her tonight. Cream asks her if she'd found Jesus and if she'd received the Holy Ghost with the evidence of speaking in tongues.

Chassaray responded, "Yes, did you?"

"Yes," she said, and they both began jumping up and down with amazement. They continued to bless the Lord throughout the night. The service started and the bishop is so excited about the word of God going forth. He says that that night's word is about "trusting God," contrary to what the enemies set out to do. The bishop is so hyped when it comes to the people of God. The bishop carries a very heavy anointing upon him, and his anointing has been very prosperous for the whole city. It has carried him all over the world from country to country. Just before the pastor begins to preach, he decides to have all the ladies stand and give a hug to all their neighbors in reference to the love of God as a stranger. The pastor explained to the women that by showing love to one another unconditionally was the way of the Lord Jesus.

Pastor Dahnogfet's explains how his ministry of love has brought back family members together from years of brokenness and loss hope. The women's expression was of awe and excitement for a connection with their neighbor in whom they never knew. Pastor Dahnognet asked the women to take about five minutes to walk around the complex and find a total stranger or the women next to them to hug and say "I love you" to. As they begin to walk around the arena to show love to one another, he explained to them how a seed of warm love indeed, as the Bible has said would bring restoration within the hearts of broken women, because it will overcome the negative energy that harbors sin from person to person. Pastor Dahnogfet said that this positive attitude of giving love at any cost tonight could be a great start for everyone with great faith and could restore back lost families, restore brokenness, and more than anything, it's a melting pot for the sinners' forgiveness without respect of person. So, as they were all wrapping up their hugs of love and returning to their seats, Chassaray and CREAM grab each other's hand and began walking back to their seats, excited and overjoyed with the presence of God. Cream slows down as she looks over and sees Romona standing at the third row sees Romona standing at the third row of seats, hugging, and weeping with another woman. She quickly looks at Chassaray and smiles at her and says, "Wow!" "What?" says Chassaray. "Look, it's Romona standing there, and she looks as if she's overjoyed with tears." Romona's standing there with tears of adoration for the lord. Chassaray is anxious trying to figure what she should do at this moment, after all, it was an hour of truth, love, and forgiveness, but most of all, she knew she had to walk in integrity in order for her seed of love to remain and grow.

Tears began to roll down Chassaray's face as she stands compelled to walk over to her and say hello just to show love, besides she knows that Romona needs love so much. Cream looks at Chassaray and began to squeeze her hand and nods her head to go to her and says to her, "Yes, go over and give her a hug. They'd just experienced great moments of joyful bliss they'd not experienced on this level before and didn't want anything to vex their spirit, so they walk a little closer to her seat. Chassaray takes a deep breath and walks over to her and taps her on her shoulder. Romona turns around with tears in her eyes.

Chassaray says to her, "I know that this situation seems a little weird, but I'm Solomon's girlfriend, and I don't mean to be rude of any kind, but I know about your secret sexual encounter with my soon-to-be fiancé."

Though Solomon hadn't gotten into the details about the day he was late picking Chassaray up, it was best that he hadn't. She had spared herself of it all because she had forgiven him. This was her character; she was a loving, nurturing, understanding young lady who has a lot to offer any respectable, deserving young man loving, nurturing, understanding young lady who has a lot to offer any respectable, deserving young man.

Chassaray says, "I found out the night it happened. There's no need to deny it, because Solomon and I have talked about it and have both gotten over it." She said, "I'd like to offer my forgiveness to you—it's what Christ would have me to do."

Chassaray hugs her, and Romona grips Chassaray's waist really tight and looks into her eyes and says to her, "I'm sorry and I know it won't change what happened that night, but I'm here as a result of the guilt I feel for being with him and hurting the both of you. "Romona, it's over, but you must have learned your lesson that having sex with any man at all, without the covenant of God Almighty in marriage is a sin and indeed a grave risk to take. I just hope that you've realized that you couldn't be standing in a better place right now at this very moment,

Romona."

Romona stands there in great anticipation while tears roll down her face. "Chassaray, my sister"—as she grabs her hand— "there's more that I must tell you!"

Cream looks at Romona and Chassaray with confusion in her eyes. Cream says, "More? Romona, I don't mean to be rude, but, honey, what more could you possibly have to say.""See, I just found out that I was HIV positive!"

"OMG! Chassaray, I'm so sorry!"

"Whaa … what … did you just say?"

"Yes, I'm HIV positive."

"Are you sure?" Chassaray asked.

"Yes," says Romona. "See, I've three boys who are very active in soccer and one of them was injured on the field with a severe kick to the kidneys and needed a blood transfusion a few days ago, so I went in to deliver for my son with this transfusion, and I was found out that I couldn't because I was positive, and now, I have to recall back the men I've slept with and their whereabouts. I've slept with so many men and some of them were married some engaged too. IT WAS ALL ABOUT THE MONEY, and I was blinded, I'm so sorry. Now, I don't know what to do because my friends and family, who claimed to love me when I was bringing money home to them from my prostitution and stripping, won't have anything to do with me."

Chassaray was broken down all over again, and she began weeping very hard, almost buckling at the knees.

Chassaray says, "We have to leave and go tell Solomon right now."

Cream says, "Chass, Chass, calm down now. We can't go running to him while you're not yourself. It just wouldn't go well for you. People just don't think rational when they're upset. So, let's just stay here and receive the word of God and while your spirit is being fed, you can gather all your thoughts."

"Okay, Cream, it makes sense."

Chassaray and Cream walk from Romona holding each other and both crying and in disbelief. She stops and turns around and asks, "How long have you known, Romona?

How could you let this happen to him?" Romona stated, "Hey! I told you, I'm a repenting prostitute who now wants more out of life. I want to convert to becoming a Jew, because I have no faith in your Jesus." "Well, if you have no faith in the love of Jesus, why are you here?"

Cream excuses herself to go find a prayer warrior quick! She's calm but doesn't know how this will end, so she takes off to get someone to pray for them both. It was already time for service to start. Cream finally sees a prayer warrior standing to the back walking toward her swiftly.

Meanwhile, Romona's still explaining to Chassaray saying, "I know it wasn't right, and I shouldn't have been sleeping around, but I fell for that lustful spirit out there in the world most people do. Now, karma, as they say, has laid wrath upon me for being so evil. It all came with the territory of being a model who does everything to make it to the top. I saw him, he looked appealing to me, and I did everything I could to get him, but that was before I found out that I was HIV positive. If I hadn't found out, I probably wouldn't have stopped, and that's the ugly truth. Cream comes back with the prayer warrior just in time to grab Chassaray before she lost her strength to stand. They can see from afar that something was wrong with Chassaray's posture. Chassaray lets out one big scream, "Nooo!"

Cream gets there and says, "Chass, it's going to be okay."

Chassaray's, standing there with her hands over her mouth, is shocked at what she's hearing. Meanwhile, Chassaray's standing there with Cream clinched to her waist. Romona's eyes looked as if they were pierced with the devil.

As all of this is taking place, the congregation has been watching. "Solomon!" she hollered out.

"He's going to die, Cream!"

"OMG!"

Chassaray didn't know how she would be telling Solomon this very disturbing and sad news. After all, he probably thought he'd never see this girl Romona again because he'd promised Chassaray that he wouldn't ever see her or any girl again. Solomon had felt as though out of all the girls he'd been with, Chassaray was indeed the one for him.

The pastor comes to the podium and calls for another moment of prayer and requested that everyone hold hands. So, the women did. He then called for the prayer warriors to bring the two ladies to the altar. As he steps down to speak to the two ladies, he notices that another young lady is moving toward the prayer warrior, Chassaray and Cream.

The pastor asks, "What must be the problem?"

"She," Chassaray cries out to the pastor. "She killed him! She killed him! We were going to spend our lives together. I ... I forgave him and took him back, but now we will never be able to sleep together and raise that family we wanted because of this prostitute."

Pastor Dagnogfet said, "Who killed him, my child?"

Chassaray, shivering, looks up to him then turns and points at Romona, who, by this time, was standing near her, drowning in tears.

Cream says, "Chassaray, calm down. We will get through this. Let's go get a drink of water."

Chassaray says, "Well, we have to be quick because I don't wanna miss the service."

As they're walking off, Cream says, "As soon as we leave here, we're gonna have to go see Solomon immediately. He's not going to believe what has happened here. More importantly, it's such a great thing that you guys never slept together. It pays to remain a virgin until you're married."

"Yes, and I'm so glad I listened to my parents. My

parents would keel over dead if they find out that I had sex. Dad is always in my spirit about all my decisions." "Cream, I'm so afraid for Solomon. Well, let's just calm our nerves right now and get through this service. It's indeed a hard situation to get used to, and there will definitely be a lot of healing emotionally and physically if he tests positive."

"Cream, do you think God will heal him, so that we can be together like we'd planned? Solomon and I had talked about living a life committed to Jesus."

"That must mean something right, Chass?"

"Well, Cream, my faith has always been in Christ's resurrection and power of any situation."

"If it's God's will, Chassaray, he will be healed indeed. There's been lots of healings from the Bible time, and even in these days we live in now. If you look at TBN, you'll see plenty of healing pastors healing and giving testimonies about those who trust in the power of Jesus. Chassaray, maybe after we find out, we can go travel to see one. What a bittersweet night." Meanwhile, back at the altar, the pastor's standing there in front of Romona.

"It's my fault, Pastor, I did it! I gave her fiancé HIV, but I didn't know that I was positive, nor did I know he was engaged. Not that it mattered. I was wrong, and I'm sorry, Pastor. Please ask the Lord to forgive me."

Pastor Dagnogfet says, "Child, you have to ask Him for yourself, with faith in Jesus and then willingly accept Him as Lord and savior so that you may follow Him and love Him."

Romona says, "Pastor, I don't believe in your Jesus, but I want to be healed. Is it possible that I can have healing, from the Holy Ghost without the accepting Jesus?"

The pastor was shocked with what he heard. He said, "The Holy Spirit came back for the messiah Jesus, as I'm so afraid for Solomon. Well, let's just calm our nerves right now and get through this service. It's indeed a hard situation to get used to, and there will definitely be a lot of healing emotionally and physically if he tests positive."

The pastor is now looking over to the crowd of prayer warriors to see what was going on. He calls for them to surround her and began praying immediately over her until he gets there. So, they did begin praying in tongues for about ten minutes. As the servants of God were awakening the young lady to bring her up closer to the pastor, she began to resent the servants as they were trying to carry her, so she begins to fuss, saying, "No! Don't take me! They'll kill me if I get rid of my powers. I can't commit to your Jesus! Noo!" So, they put the young lady down, not demanding anything from her because Christians aren't to be pushy. Truth is that the Holy Spirit will only come into a willing vessel. She stands up and walks over to the pastor. Appearing very sweaty and drained standing before him, shaking and ashamed, she says to Pastor Dagnotfret, "I feel some kind of way right now, Pastor, I don't know what has happened to me, and I don't know what to say, but I know you must get on with your show tonight." "Show?" he says. "My child, this is a ministry for uplifting Jesus, for He's indeed the head, therefore we follow His character with love in our spirits." Pastor Dagnogfret continues,

"Child, what is your name once more?"

"Romona, Pastor."

"Well, Romona, Jesus is very real, just as you're standing here, and if you desire to be healed as much as you desired to not believe in Him, by faith, you must believe in Him to be blessed from heaven. Your will, Romona. It's in your will! Romona stands there, bowed down very lowly in spirits, and her small, petite physical posture seemed frail and worn out with life from all the running game with men and sleeping around. "Pastor, I will stay. I'll stay and listen to your message, and I've faith that you have the power from Christ in heaven to heal me from this HIV."

"Okay then, very well, Romona. Go to your seat, then after this service, we will call for healing at the altar."

The time now is 8:00 pm, and the pastor is finally able to start preaching. As he's preaching, the anointing begins to hit him very hard, and he gets a rhema word from God to call all who were HIV positive at that time to come to the altar for healing. Now, this arena seats about 2,500 people at a time, and almost half the women there came up for a healing. They were all astonished at each other, looking at one another in a lovely shame as they filed down to the altar.

Surprised at the faces that were approaching the altar, they weep and instantly began calling on Jesus saying,

"Mercy, mercy!" Since God lead him to heal surprisingly after only about fifteen minutes of preaching that night, he obeyed God. One by one he anointed them and lay hands on them, and they all left the altar grateful and praising God and believing for their healing. This amazing testimony has addressed the women of most societies of how they're just too careless with their health when it comes to emotional decisions versus the controlling, pompous egos of most men, which almost always lead to sin and disaster for her.

Well, the service was over about 10:30 p.m., and Chassaray and Cream headed out of the arena fast to Cream's house.

"Chassaray, you really need to ask Jehovah God to help you for the strength to be calm and wise when you're speaking because although you've forgiven him, it's now a sore spot, a very hard conversation to get through."

"Okay, Cream. I'll try my best to be strong. I don't know what I'd do without you, Cream."

They hugged each other and tell how much they appreciate each other and that they're glad to have had the parents that they've had who certainly raised them to be dedicated to Christ.

"All right, my friend, I must go now, I'll call you in the am."

"Okay, good night."

The next morning at 9:00 a.m. on Friday at the firm, Cream walks into the foyer headed to the elevator and is startled by a voice calling out of the elevator. It opens back up. It was Romona. "Cream, Cream!" she calls out. "Uhmm. Hi! How are you today?"

Very sternly, Cream stands with an amazed but disgusted look on her face as if Romona shouldn't have been there. She walks over to Cream and as if she wanted to hug her, but Cream stepped back. "What do you want, Romona? Look, Romona, I know that you're feeling ashamed, and mainly, because you're showing up here at our place of work is just intrusive and out of character."

"Sister Cream, I can understand your pain right now, but may I please have your forgiveness please, especially for my turned-up actions displayed last night of laughing while you guys stood there in pain. Cream, I could hardly sleep last night thinking of all the pain that I've caused everyone."

"Uhm, Sister Cream, I'm here to speak with Chassaray, have you seen her?"

"She's not here just yet, Romona, and I think it would be best if you not come here for an apology, it's very inappropriate. Now, if you can leave your number and I'll have her to contact you if she so desires."

"But, Cream, I'm already here, and I just wanted to explain to you and Chassaray that besides getting prayed for, a really great transformation appeared last night. Cream, I put my trust in the Lord for my healing and salvation. So, I'm believing that the test results are going to be different this time around, and that means that I'm hoping the same for Solomon. I suggest that maybe we get him to a priest or a bishop for healing, so that hands are laid upon him."

"Oh, Cream, please enlighten me. Don't you agree that last night was bittersweet. We all came looking for something, one thing perhaps, but we were fed another."

"Cream, I've given into Jesus, who I didn't believe in, and it was all because of my ignorance of that I was in the dark for so long. I'm healed, and if you can find it in your heart to forgive me and allow me to be your sister in Christ this day, it would certainly make my day. I don't care that it makes me look like I'm begging you. The truth is that I have no real friends anymore because everyone I ran with or thought I could trust all walked away when I told them about my diagnosis. My very best friend since kindergarten warned me that she would leave me if I would keep stripping, gambling, stealing, and hurting other people—period. I wouldn't listen because I thought … I'm a grown woman, and it didn't matter if our friendship ended at this point because the money was too good. Well, this pretty much is, Cream, I have nothing more to hide from the world anymore. I can't hurt any more than I am right now. I'm an open book. So will you accept, Cream?"

"Romona, I'm not gonna stand here and discredit your faith at this point because I know it took a great deal of strength to step out like you did last night and today as well, and I applaud you and encourage you to continue growing in Christ. I'll just let you know that I do accept your friendship invitation and will talk to Chassaray today, and we'll give you a call later. Maybe we can get together and have some coffee at Starbucks." Cream walks over to Romona and gives her a hug, and says, "God bless you." Romona, walks off. Heading toward the front door, she sees Solomon off a distance and wondered if she should stop him and talk to him, but she wondered if Chassaray had had a chance to speak with him about the situation. Romona took off fast out of the door toward the bridge walkway to meet up with Solomon and talk to Solomon; she couldn't resist the chance to tell him the news. So, she calls out Solomon. He responds saying, "Yes, Romona what are you doing here? This is my place of business, what are you doing here?"

She instantly broke out in tears after seeing his face again. She fell in his arms and told him, "I'm sorry, Solomon.

I'm sorry for hurting you and Chassaray."

Solomon is looking at her like, "What are you talking about?"

Romona looks up at Solomon and says, "Please say that you won't lose your mind."

"Okay, Romona, what … what is it?"

"Well, I was put in a situation with one of the kids recently that had gotten hurt during a soccer game, and I had to be a blood donor for him, and that's when I found out that I was HIV positive, Solomon."

Solomon couldn't believe what he was hearing; his

heart almost stopped.

"You got ... what! How long have you known this, Romona? Woman, you're lying!"

"No, I'm not, Solomon."

"You dirty greedy little skunk, how could you not let me know this beforehand? Did someone put you up to this? Oh, I get it! You're a part of that gang or circle of secret friends who does whatever for money around here? I should've known just by looking at you: You have chicalet teeth, and you could care less about you alopecia. **YOU CARE ABOUT NOTHING BUT MONEY!!!!!! JEZEBEL!!!"** Solomon was enraged."Solomon! Will you stop fussing? I'm trying to come clean here! Listen, I just found out last week. I wanted to call you last week and tell you, but I couldn't because I was too ashamed. I didn't know what to say and who to talk to, and I finally realized I needed some type of spiritual strength, so that's when I'd heard of the ladies' conference coming up during this week at the arena. I had a talk with the pastor, and he anointed me and laid hands upon me and prayed for my healing."

"Arena? Arena! You went last night, Romona?"

"Yes, and, Solomon, I did bump into your girlfriend Chassaray. She and Cream walked over to me to hug me as the pastor asked us all to."

"What! So, you guys had your own little conference about me last night. So, Romona, how did that work for you, being that you know Chassaray loves me and we were gonna get engaged very soon? OMG! Romona, how could you do this and in such an inappropriate place."

"Well, after last night, I thought about all the greedy, deceitful intentions I had to get anything or any man I wanted in life. Solomon, I wanted change very badly! Just as much as I was hungry for the evil in the world, I became very hungry for something more. I'd always used my manipulative ways, of the laws of attraction, and it never mattered how much I'd hurt anyone else, especially those I envied. My last relationship was with a man who I knew was involved and loved by a good friend of mine. I pretended that I didn't know him and that it was an accident. I didn't even care. I just wanted him, and nothing was going to stop me from getting him, and now it's come down to this—he could've been my downfall. I stole her joy and broke her heart and watched her cry for a year. I hid from her, hoping that she never found out where I was. I tormented her spiritually. If I saw her getting close to him, I would block her spiritually, and I know that God didn't like that. I hated her because she was beautiful naturally without all the fake lashes and boobs. I was always doing dirty deeds while doing good for the community as well. I thought I could never get bad karma. I didn't know this guy was HIV positive, and he never told me. He invited me into activities that lead to me making lots of money, including a drug ring down in Florida. We fell in love for a short period. I thought we were in love, and we got in engaged in spite of his infidelity to me because of the porn industry we were involved in. I went along with him sleeping around, and he didn't mind if I did the same. We all slept around with each other in the group. We weren't a part of the gang, but we knew of them. We even went as far as worship the devil himself— it became a cult. There were blood sacrifices, just as the Illuminati. We actually called up demons for power and strength just like them. The third eye was opened where we would know exactly every move of our enemies and could cut them off, block them, and even go into their homes and intrude their privacy, mind controlling their lives to make bad things happen to them. Solomon, it was horrible! I mean, really horrible."

SHOULD YOU EVEN BE NEAR THE CHURCH?? (This is a very important question, that most DARK lost souls want to know and are too afraid to ask). MATTHEW 18:1-18 *7.) I say unto you, that likewise joy shall be in heaven over one sinner that repent, more than over ninety and nine just persons, which need no repentance.

"Why didn't you tell me your evil heart had this much darkness in it? OMG! How could I not discern this?" Solomon says. "This is what I get for being so mindless and superficial."

"Well, that is the problem with most men today."

"Romona! I know you're not standing there being sarcastic. Slut!"

"You're right, Solomon! I will agree I was a slut, but I've changed, and I don't wanna go back to darkness. So, I gotta stay away from the same people who allowed all this to happen without a conscience. This circle has grown with over thousands of members across the United States, unknown by most. It's a corporate move full of schemes to make money, which is why there are rich CEOs at the top. All the time I was running with these guys, traveling around the world from island to island and state to state with this disease in my body. This disease is now my karma, and if it's not cured, I can never have sex again. So, I'm the one who actually loses. I guess Jehovah God really is in control of this world. Even though I'd chosen my God in the world as the universe and the powers of darkness because I didn't wanna believe in the son of God, after my son was hurt in the soccer accident. I grew very curious and burdened with the guilt of my own bloody hands. My karma had come back to hunt me through my kids, now me. I'm sorry, and I do understand if you're upset, but I actually ran into Chassaray and Cream by accident at the conference last night. It was a coincidence, but it was greatly divine intervention. We talked, we were all prayed for, and I admitted everything to them and the pastor. Solomon, you have to understand that we have to figure out what do we do from here. Well, I'm believing in the healing that was performed for me last night on the altar, although I'm still going to the doctor's office today as a walk-in to have more test ran, and I'll let you know at that point where I stand. Meanwhile, you should get tested and maybe see a healing pastor."

Solomon didn't say much. He just stood in disbelief, looking at her and reminiscing about the promiscuity from his past. If he'd not found Chassaray, then he very well could've passed the virus to a lot of other girls but being so excited thinking that Chassaray is the one for him, and he hadn't been with anyone else since Romona. He just stood there thinking of how he was willing to change his life for Chassaray this time, and now this was all going to just be a dream. He's lost it all for a one-night stand with a prostitute. All he could think of was how he was going to be able to talk to Chassaray about his disgusting past. He was so afraid because he knew Chassaray was one of those stern types who made her decisions very clear. She made her own money and certainly didn't need him, although she loved him very much. Chassaray had given him two chances when he'd cheated with two women. Abby and Romona, and now the sex with the hot Romona was coming back to haunt him. He was definitely becoming weak and feeling very useless right now.

Solomon couldn't even go in to work that day, so he turned around and headed to his apartment and on the way home called in to work with an emergency. He speeded down the highway, crying tears and repenting with God not to let it be true. Promising to not ever be promiscuous again and if God would heal him, he's give his life to God and serve Jesus the rest of his days. Solomon knew his modeling career would be over. Let alone his nine-to-five job, and his reputation was over. Solomon gets home and calls his parents and explains to them everything. His mother and father were very disappointed and hurt.

She wept very hard and almost got to the point where she wanted to go find this young lady and give her a piece of her mind, but she remembers that she was saved and that she knows that the Lord has vengeance above evil. She wanted to know where to find this young lady, but she quickly regained her composure for Solomon's sake. She tells him to come over so that he can be near his family.

He goes over to his parents' house and just falls to pieces explaining to them how he was getting really serious with Chassaray and they'd talked about engagement soon. This surprised his parents as well.

His dad says, "Let's make an appointment right now at Cedar Sinai Hospital in about two hours. Okay, Solomon, son, your mom has always told you about these promiscuous women, which is why we've spent so much time teaching you about the principles of the Bible and put you in the highest quality of schools so that you may acquire a companion of great quality! Not some prostitute off the street, Solomon. You have the intelligence and credentials to get you anywhere in life. You had a beautiful life."

"OMG! I can't believe this is happening to our son. This is just like a shot to my own heart. I raised my son to be better than this. Solomon, what are you gonna do with your modeling career? No one's going to want you on the cover of anything!" said Solomon's mother.

"Yeah, I know, Mom. Well, Mom, I promise you one thing. It's this: No matter what happens, I'm going to commit my life to the Lord Jesus. Mom and Dad, I'm sorry for the embarrassment that it's going to cause you."

"We love you, son, and we're always going to be here for you, no matter. We'll never stop."

"No, son, never. We'd better be get going. We don't wanna run into bad traffic." It's 12:00 p.m., and the hospital is crowded. Solomon and his family arrive to there as a walk-in hoping to be seen today. Since it's been at least a couple of months since Solomon had slept with Romona, they're hoping for a miracle by chance. Mrs. Koldinaldo goes to the window and ask for Dr. Lowe for a walk-in appointment for today, and the secretary looks to see if he's in today.

"Why, yes, Mrs. Koldinaldo, he's here, but he's running behind schedule. Do you mind waiting for an hour while we fit you in?"

"No, we don't mind."

An hour and a half passes, and the Koldinaldos are called in for their visit. Dr. Lowe was kind of curious as to why the entire family was there in one day.

"Well, Dr. Lowe, we've some bad news that we're hoping not to be true for our son."

"What seems to be the matter, Karen?"

"Solomon has slept around with a hot prostitute, and she just found out she's HIV positive."

"Christ!" he says. "Solomon, my boy, I've known you since you were a kid. What's going on that you feel that you didn't need protection?"

"Nothing," as he burst into tears.

"Have you guys talked to your pastor yet?"

"No, we haven't yet. I guess we should as soon as possible ask for prayer, healing, and repentance," says Solomon's mom.

Solomon says, "Mom, I'm not so sure that telling him would be wise. He'll just treat me as a black sheep."

"Well, you are a black sheep at this point. You've gone out to act as if you have no home training and standards, and you act as if you've never been taught biblical principles. Well, let's get this blood drawn for test, and we'll see about getting Solomon into some safe-sex abstinence classes. It will take twenty-four hours for the test to come back. I should know something by 2:00 p.m. tomorrow. Please give me your cell number, and I will call you with the results, or you can call me."

Solomon goes home with his family and stays there until Chassaray gets off work just thinking about what he's going to say to her. Chassaray had called several times during lunch, but Solomon had his ringer turned off. He turned it off on purpose because he didn't want Chassaray to say it was over. So, she calls again at 5:00 p.m., and he finally picks up.

Solomon was surprised at her attitude and concern about his whereabouts and how he was doing. He was relieved.

"Chassaray, Chassaray, oh my darling, it's so good to hear your voice."

"Solomon, are you okay? Where are you right now?"

"I'm at my mom's house."

"Why?"

"Well, I guess I shouldn't ask that question. I have to talk to you, and I have to talk you today. It's urgent!"

"Chassaray, what's wrong?" he asked.

"I need you to meet me at DRILLOS Bar and Lounge at 7:00 pm."

"Okay! All right."

"All right, Chassaray, see ya then."

Solomon decides to let some steam out, so he heads to the gym, and he sees REGAN. REGAN doesn't know about what happened, so Solomon tells him that he's hit rock bottom and definitely needs his support.

"REGAN, man, I've really gotta a bomb to drop."

"What up, man?"

"Man, remember that chick Romona that I met at club DRILLOS? Well, man, this girl comes to me today and tells me that she just found out that she's HIV positive."

REGAN gets hysterical. "What! Man, you didn't protect yourself? I told you, you can't be messing with all these females. Some of them are disgusting and scandalous when it comes to making a penny, and they'll take you down with them. Did you actually pay for sex? You can get any girl you want, why would you?"

"Well, REGAN, I didn't. She never told me she was

a greenbow prostitute until afterward. Man, she drop the bomb on me about who she was and how she rolled with her crew."

"OMG! Man, I was speechless because I knew I was a Casanova, but usually kinda mindful or discerning about the chicks that I pick."

"My brother, this one caught me off guard. It was like she'd used some kind of charm she used to lure me into her."

REGAN says, "Man, she may have used some ungodly, demonic powers, who knows. Maybe she was even sent to you specifically just because you're rich."

"Yep, REGAN, you're right because she told me that she and her friends would worship the devil by selling their souls for dark powers. She said they'd use mind control to get what they wanted from anyone."

"Jesus Christ, Solomon. You have to be more careful, and what can we do about all this. These evil people need to be handled, my man." "Exactly, you're right, because it's a corporate scheme that will cause the entire world to fall victim to these savage villains. They're going to ruin the Christian faith in Jesus when people look at them and how they're accomplishing their success to quicker and it works, but, Solomon, these are the powers of darkness at work in the minds of thousands and maybe millions of people. Solomon, I can't believe this is happening to you, brother, and the world's ain't ready for the evil that has been unleashed by these evil broods. My God! Solomon,

I feel for you. You're my brother, and I'll do anything to help you, but I just know that we're going to have to be very wise about the entire situation."

"Well, I did get the blood test done today. So, my life depends on this test. Tomorrow, I'll have the results. Tonight, I'm meeting Chassaray at Drillos Bar and Lounge."

"Solomon, my brother, please be very wise about your conversations and don't let it get out of control. Remember, God is in control, so if it's meant to be, it will last through the good and bad. Who knows, maybe God will put it in her heart to keep you, pray for you, and protect you for life."

"Man, do you think he'll do that for me? I've been such a horrible person disrespecting women by sexing them without committing in marriage. All this fornication of sin has caught up with me. Regan, I prayed and repented already, but I plan to go but hell without him. I mean this. Regan, I wonder if the guys that she rolls with knows Sommers and her friend Simone who wanted to date Novis and Jacob."

"No one ever heard from Summers since she was hospitalized. I'm wondering if she recovered from her coma." Solomon says, "Well, I did hear that Sommers was out of her coma, but she's indeed still badly sick with her diabetes, but she's back to her scheming again."

"Yes, Solomon, these chicks are bad business and are certainly beneath our stature, and maybe they're involved with Romona as well. Recalling the story, you told about her money ring to the feds immediately. Sommers is into mind control, has third eye, and witchcraft the whole nine yards too. We've got to find out and report this to the Feds as soon as possible."

"I know, and we have to be smart about it, because these are demons we're dealing with. It's almost as if we'd have to connect with an evil entity ourselves just to outwit them. No!" said Solomon. "I got a feeling also that Novis and Jacob could help us out here. Let's play it smart, maybe we can use them as bait or something to get into the circle and find out information indirectly without them knowing themselves."

"Solomon, man, that sounds like deceit, and that's bound to take us back into another layer of sin. If these guys knew that we were deceiving them, they'd never trust us again. After all, I've known them personally for years. They are already weird and wild, and we don't wanna lose them trying to find answers to a perpetual case that could be a cycle of aimless taunts from Satan himself. Solomon, we need the power of Jesus for real. I'm talking sleepless priest (lol) and prayer warriors around the world. Okay, then that's what we'll do, but when you talk to Chassaray, make sure that you mention to her that this situation bigger and badder than we know right now. Solomon to our pastor about the spirits that are a hindrance to me and my life—period. I'm saying I'm ready to get saved, man. There's nothing else out here, man. With Chassaray, I've found all I need in a woman. I'm young, I'm twenty-five, but I'm already tired. It's time to grow up and live for Jesus. Life is too precious with him give her my love."Cream calls Chassaray at 6:00 pm to meet her for their girls' day out time today, and Chassaray asks her to come with her to talk to Solomon at 7:00 pm. Cream said that she thought that she should go alone and that she just go hang out with REGAN, so that they can go talk about their engagement as well. Chassaray says, "Well, this is a big day for both of you, and I respect that. Well, I'll just talk to you later, like tomorrow. Hopefully, you guys can come to an understanding, because I know you love him."

"I love you so much, Chassaray! God bless you, sis. Remember we're Christians, and the power of the Holy Ghost is within us and helps us to manage our problems with discretion and godly wisdom. So even if we hear negative results tomorrow, then Solomon still has us for support and encouragement. It's the kingdom's way. Others in the world may choose otherwise, but we're not going to turn away from him now. He'll need us more than ever."

"Okay, good night, sis."

"Oh, Chassaray, I almost forgot that Romona came by the job this morning asking to talk to you, but I told her that we'd give her a call and maybe we could all meet up with her. What do you think?"

"Well, I think that I definitely needed more time before seeing her again because of how she just laughed about the situation. I wouldn't have spoken to her first thing this morning. Well, let's pray that there's some type of miracle happening for them both. Cream, this is all so hard for me because it's going to affect my job performance just worrying about him and how he's doing because of this chick. Cream, the more I think about it, the angrier I get, and it becomes harder for me to want to forgive. I know we were prayed up, delivered, and filled with the Holy Spirit last night, but what must a woman of such great prestige do when her trust and faith is being tested more than ever just when she wanted to believe more and give her life totally and completely to Jesus. I knew that if the dedication and commitment on both our behalf was there, we would definitely be on fire for the Lord. Okay, I gotta stop thinking about it and go talk to my dad about it." "What, your dad? Okay, this isn't a job for a superhero." "Come on, Cream, give me a break." "Aight, it was just small sarcasm. Okay, well here's her number. If you so desire to call her afterward, then you can." "Okay, thanks. I'll see you later and call me as soon as you get done." It's Friday back at the firm and it's time for Mr. Moolunrig and Mr. Higgins to host a yearly men's function for the prestigious men of honor, so they're back at the office discussing about Solomon and Regan. They were both chosen to stand before other great men of stature who had opened doors by contributing to the company's stock asset fund for potential young immigrant business owners. The company has been very successful capitalizing off stock with the company. Well, this has been the company's operating system, which has been a great blessing to the community. Faith Law Firm has also been quite instrumental in supporting and benefiting the sick as well as the homeless around the city. So as dedicated and hard-working men in the company, these two men were chosen to go out and compete as the company's representatives to feed and fund their chosen organizations.

Mr. Higgins called Solomon to tell him of the good news that just came across in a meeting with Mr. Moolunrig. Solomon picks up on the fourth ring. "Hello?" in a heavy, groggy voice, he answered.

Solomon had been on his mom's couch enjoying Sangria Mimosa lime wine until he was almost tipsy. So, when he answered the phone, he realized he'd almost missed his meeting time with Chassaray. It was almost 6:15 p.m., and he was to be there at 7:00 pm. Solomon knew this call had to be very short.

He answered, "Mr. Higgins! What a pleasant surprise to hear from you. How are things at the firm?"

"Well, Solomon, you and Regan have been chosen to represent the company as 'Men of Prestige' year-round award." Laughing very loudly, Mr. Higgins says, "Son, isn't that great?"

"Why, yes, of course."

Says Mr. Higgins, "Now, you'll just need to be here on tomorrow morning. Other men trailblazers will show you how to receive your award at the ceremony and then a speech shall be spoken."

"Mr. Higgins, I've some very, very sad news."

Suddenly, he stops laughing and asks Solomon, "What's wrong, son?"

Solomon starts to cry and says, "I'm sick, Eric. I'm sick, and I'm never going to be okay."

"Son, calm down. What exactly is the ailment that you're so distraught about?"

"See, Mr. Higgins, I had a one-night stand with a girl named Romona, and it turned out to be the worst thing I could've ever done. She wasn't the classiest or the most intelligent, that I've has ever known. Mr. Higgins, this girl was a prostitute."

"What!" said Mr. Higgins. "My Lord, son."

"Yes, she was very promiscuous, and not only that, she's claiming to be positive for HIV."

"What! Oh, God, no! Solomon, have you told your parents?"

"Yes, and we went to the hospital for a testing today. Anyway, I have to go now, because I have to meet Chassaray at the lounge for a meeting. Well, the results are in tomorrow and I'll be in touch."

"Okay, son, I'm so sorry this is happening to you. Maybe, I should tell Mr. Moolunrig about this, son."

"No. Not yet, sir. I'd like to talk to him and Chassaray together."

"Okay, Solomon, just call us if there's anything we can do. Good-bye, son."

Meanwhile, Chassaray is at the bar and lounge. She's very anxious about her meeting with Solomon as she sits there contemplating on what she should say or ask him.

She decided to buy a couple of wine drinks to help calm her nerves. All she could do was sit there and think about how disrespectful and inconsiderate Solomon had been. Solomon arrives, and as soon as he sees her sitting over near the bar, he—with glasses at her—stands there and takes a deep breath and walks over to her, assuming that she must be feeling the worst, sitting here all alone.

"Chassaray," he calls.

She looks up at him pulls her shades down and pierced "Hi" with her red swollen eyes. Tears began to roll down her baby face.

"I'm sorry, Chassaray, for being late. I'd got a phone call from Mr. Higgins, and he wanted to tell me that Regan and I was selected for the prestigious 'Man of the Year' award. I was excited about that, it's a great accomplishment. Well, Chassaray—"as he looked over into her eye, which looked so hurt. He stops abruptly and says, "I'm so sorry, baby! I'm sorry I hurt you, Chassaray, I've done something that no one can ever fix except God. I didn't mean for any of this to happen. Forgive me." he cries out to her as he walks over to hug her.

"Solomon, what did you expect was going to happen, especially if you knew she was a community fling, Solomon. My God! You took our engagement and love and threw it all away for a one-night stand. Just look at how she dresses—that was enough to tell you something right there about her." "It wasn't her body nor her clothes at this point that got my attention. It was a story of how she had lost her mom from a heart attack when she was a little kid and became very defiant toward the world. She smooth talked me, sweetheart! I know there's no excuse for any of this regardless. I should've used my heart and not my mind." He stands there after talking and looks her in her eyes quietly, and Chassaray rises up in front of him and says, "Do you believe in Jesus, Solomon?"

"Well, yes, I very well do, but what does that have to do with the fact that I'm more than likely infected with HIV?" "OMG! I can't believe you actually don't have the slightest idea where I'm coming from. Solomon, we've been together long enough that you should know what my demeanor is in life. You know that I'm a Christian, right? Well, Cream and I both were filled with the Holy Spirit, with the evidence of speaking in tongues, which is why I'm asking you this. I was baptized as kid, and now I wanna go a little further in my relationship with God, so I'm asking you the question would you like to give your heart to Jesus as Lord as and savior. I mean, if we were going to get engaged, you would've had to do it anyway. So, this present circumstance should be the perfect time to do so even the more, don't you think?"

"Yes, Chassaray. I need Him really bad right now."

"Well, Solomon"—as she looks at him in his eye— "if you truly believe and commit, maybe He will heal you. Solomon, if you want, we can go back to the conference tomorrow night together."

"Sure, Chassaray, I'll go. I love you, Chassaray, and I'm hoping that God will give me this miracle either way."

"Solomon, Romona came by the office this morning wanting to see me, and Cream basically told her that it was inappropriate for her to be coming around my job to speak to me so soon. I would've agreed with her at this point. I mean, we don't even have the results yet, or what if we'd already been engaged, I mean, I'm not totally blaming her, but she's at fault for the death trap if it's true. You know, Solomon, I don't know if you can sense it, but I've been taking it very well, and this has to be God by all means. If so, I have to obey His spiritual liberty to stay calm in this."

"Okay, so we can leave around 6:00 p.m."

"Okay, and, Solomon, I'll pick you up okay."

"Okay, see you then ..."

"Oh, Romona spoke to Cream about wanting to apologize to me and make amends for our relationship, when there's absolutely nothing else that she can do to help. She left her number for me to call her and talk to her personally. So, Solomon, do you think that we should get together and talk with her after we have the results."

"OMG! It's a good thing that you two didn't see each other on a second occasion so soon beyond church, because you probably would've fought."

"Jesus Christ, Solomon, what you don't realize is that it could've happened last night at the conference in front of everyone, but I will be the better woman here."

"What! Oh, you know what, sweetheart, don't even tell me what she said last night. Let's just concentrate on the both of us getting closer to Jesus rather than what can drive a bigger wedge between us. Chassaray, do you still love me?"

"Well, of course, I still love you, Solomon. What sense would it make to stop loving you now? Jesus never stopped loving even the very people who betrayed him. I'll stand still and be a real woman of God about it and a true friend indeed, but there's only one thing, Solomon, before you leave. I really think that we should be honest with ourselves and break off the engagement. I mean, if we're being truthful about the commands of God, it says that marriage is until sickness and health, which means I shouldn't go into a marriage that is destined from the start being unhealthy with pain and suffering. Our differences are clear right now what we know that friendship could be the only alternative."

"Chassaray, if you leave me, I don't know what I will do. You're all I ever wanted in a girl." "Solomon, let's talk about this later. You should get going so that you can get yourself together for tonight."

"Please, Chassaray!"

"Solomon, I'm being honest with you, I can't go beyond the commands and wisdom of God." "Okay, Chassaray, I'll go for now, but just know that I can't handle seeing you with another man."

"Excuse me, Solomon? What did you just say? Are you telling me that there's a part of you that will resent my wishes or do anything to destroy me? Solomon, you're scaring me right now. Solomon, please let's just get our minds wrapped around this conference tonight. So again, I'll pick you up at six thirty tonight." "Okay," Solomon says. So, Solomon goes home and talks to his parents about the conference, and they are excited that he has chosen to go and receive a miracle healing, and most importantly, give his life to God. His mother asks if he would like for them to ride along with him there, but he insists that he and Chassaray should ride alone.

So, Mr. Koldinaldo says, "Well, son, if you insist on going with just the two of you alone, then we will not intervene, but your mother and I would still like to come and give the Lord some praise in advance for the miracle we're all hoping for. Son, we're on pins and needles here too." "Okay, fine, Dad, go ahead and come. I suspect the more love, the better."

Solomon gives his parents a hug and runs upstairs to look for an outfit. As Solomon's upstairs, getting ready, the strangest things started to happen. He started to feel weak and lightheaded, and his body started to jolt. It was his spirit beginning to shift into another spiritual realm as well as Romona, the spiritual witch who had promise to never use earthly powers again to hurt anyone or to connect with evil entities, but she had decided that she couldn't take it anymore. She had relapsed and forsaken the Holy Spirit called on other spirits to reach him. So, Solomon is standing there as his spirit jolts. It was the strangest thing he'd ever felt. He stares in the mirror and suddenly hears a whisper calling in his ear, saying,

"Solomon, I want you." He thought he was hearing things, so he decided to step back to open the window and come back to the mirror. At this point, he's starting to sweat, and many thoughts are going through his mind. "Did I really just hear someone call my name?"

He looks in the closet then goes back into the mirror, and she calls again his name softly and his body starts to shake and sweat uncontrollably. He panics but instead of running downstairs to tell his parents, he answers back to her, "Who's there? "Solomon, I want you. My soul longs for you, and I won't live without you." Solomon stands there and says, "WHAT? What did you just say? And who are you?" "Romona!" she answered. "Will you come be with me? We can have a great life together, and I will live to please you."

Solomon was standing there in disbelief. "Where are you, and why are you connecting with me in the spiritual realm? What is this, Romona? What kind of games are you playing?" "Solomon, it's not a game but a certain spiritual connection."

"Romona, please leave me alone, because this sounds like some old witchcraft you're using. No one with the Holy Ghost speaks to people this way except God approves, and right now, you're being selfish. You know I'm in love with Chassaray, why do you connect with me and insist on breaking us up. You've done enough and so have I. So please leave us alone. I made a simple mistake choosing to sleep with you, and you have no remorse to how you've made her feel or even me. Where's the respect for yourself?"

"Gone, Solomon! It's gone, and yes, I broke my promises to God, and now, I can't go back to living for Him so I'm going to do what I know works for me and that's to love you and live for you. I'll cook for you, give you massages, steal for you—heck, I'll even kill for you if you leave Chassaray. Come with me, and I'll show you how we can become rich and take over the world."

Solomon's standing there with his hands clutched into a shirt he'd pulled out of the closet. He's shaking, and suddenly, he just blanks out and falls unto his bed into an hour forty-five-minute nap then wakes up and realizes he has only an hour to get dressed before Chassaray arrives. He's jumps up and runs to the shower, and as he is showering, it becomes very steamy in the bathroom, so he

hops out the shower and looks in the mirror and sees his face, and it looked as if his pupils were enlarged and blackened, so he wipes the mirror to see if he was just tripping.

As he wipes even more, he starts to panic, breathing hard, and suddenly, a woman appears, and he turns around and it's Romona.

She has come to invite him once more to join her into the darkness. Romona says, "We can move to Miami, Florida, and raise a family, and I can show you how to become rich with magic. My baby daddy's mom has moved there, and she's into the church and knows God, so we can really get this thing planned out. I mean, we can really grow a huge regime of savage, money-hungry people who are sorcerers, witches, and wizards all across the East Coast that are willing and able to fight for money at all cause. Solomon, our regime can be unstoppable, and, baby, we already are because we tried this on someone else before and they died. We can take over the kingdom of God and have people following us and they won't even know that we're scheming for money because we will look just like we're hungry and searching for truths, but we will be steadfast, and we won't give up until we get all the money we want and become rich."

"Romona, are you insane!" "No! I'm not. I'm a witch who wants you and I'll stop at nothing to have you." "Romona, I thought you went back to the church to get back your relationship with God and Jesus."I did, but after going home and hanging around everyone else who seemed so happy without Jesus, I said to myself I can't do this because I love money and the only way to become rich is if I rob and kill others for it." "What? You are the devil, Romona, and I can't even believe I slept with you, and now that I've been with you, there's a soul tie and I know you and your people will just keep stalking me if I don't give you what you want, but I'm sorry to tell you, Romona, Chassaray's on her way here now to pick me up for church tonight. Just because this happened it doesn't mean that we're breaking up! Besides, I wouldn't want to give my soul to the devil just for any amount of money."

"Hey!" said Romona! "Listen, how about this, I can make you invisible, and we can time travel together and do anything to anyone. You can even make people do what you want them to do. You can even make bad court cases go away, get out of jail, even win the lottery. Solomon, please!"

"Noooo! Romona, now please just leave here however you got here the same way. I don't even know why I'm talking to you right now."

"Solomon," she screeches out his name in a very angry voice. "If you don't, I will kill Chassaray and steal her soul and become like her and be rich. I'll steal the blueprint of her life and make her miserable."

"Romona! Leave!"

And *poof*, just like that, she disappears and runs out of the bathroom and puts a chair in front of the door with a Bible in the seat of the chair. Solomon jumps across the bed to get to the closet to get his outfit out. Stumbling and racing to get his clothes on, he's hysterical, and it still has not dawned on him about what has just occurred. Chassaray pulls up and hears Chassaray coming in the house. Solomon races downstairs to meet Chassaray. He kisses her and grabs her hand. Shaking his head while looking at her and his mother, he starts to stutter and explain to them about Romona who had just showed up in his room to invite him into fornication and all sorts of evil with her.

Mrs. Kaldinaldo says, "How did she come in here without me letting her in?"

"No! Mom, she's a witch, and she came through the

spiritual realm in my room then my bathroom. Mom! It's serious. This chick is crazy. She says that if I don't be with her, she's going to kill Chassaray."

"OMG! We have to hurry to the church and tell the pastor about this. This is sick and creepy! Yes, Lord!" Mrs. Kaldinado is screaming to her husband. "Honey, let's go. We have to get going in a hurry, there's some serious issues that we must alert the pastor about tonight preferably before the conference starts."

"Well, I don't think we'll make it there that soon. We're definitely going to have to get a watchman over our son's life."

"Sweetheart, what happened? I'll tell you about it on the way to the conference. Let's go."

They all leave in two different cars trailing each other to the conference. So, Mrs. Kaldinaldo starts to tell Mr. Kaldinaldo about Solomon being shaken up even the more with this girl Romona's behavior.

"Well," said Mrs. Kaldinaldo, "you're surely not going to believe what this child has gotten himself into now." "What?" said Mr. Kaldinaldo.

"He has slept with Satan and didn't even know it."

"OMG! What are you saying, he slept with the devil?"

"Well, Solomon says that this chick Romona just

appeared or teleported to him in his room and bathroom."

"What? No, are you kidding me? What kind of mess is

that? What kind of person is this chick?" "Well, apparently, honey, she's some type of witch or something. Most of these young kids are these days. They're either wiccan, witches, or in some cult. Lord, help us! Help my son! Solomon should've come downstairs and told us about her drifting into our home like that, she could've put some type of spell on our home. From what I've heard about these cults and gangs, when one comes, there's always more to follow. Always! They mostly travel in packs."

"OMG! You're right, honey, and I wonder if this girl has anything to do with that case of the young rapper whose home was busted for drugs, only to find out that he had been pimping women through his home for at least fifteen years, several females were found in the home at the time beaten and drugged up."

"My God, someone needs to help bring these kids to Jesus quick, before there's no turning back eternally! What are these young people thinking about? Honey, we need to do something for these kids, but first, we have to talk to the pastor about our own family's healing and protection."

"Yes, dear! You're right. We have to do something, but we need to make sure our son is well protected before we take on any new endeavors or community projects. This is crazy, and I will not have this young lady ruining my son's life or ours. He's made a dramatic change by not going out to the clubs or drinking anymore, and now, because of this one female, we may end up losing our son forever to death. We have to do something quick that will stop her in her tracks. There's no telling what she's planning or doing right now. Well, for starters, we're going to have to go to the pastor and ask that he pray for us as well and ask for our soul protection and spiritual impartation. We will need a great deal more of the Holy Ghost and also Christian warriors to help us pray against these demonic forces." "Okay."

They all finally make it to the convention center just as the praise team was about to start, so Mrs. Kaldinaldo suggested that she and her husband go behind the scenes of things to talk to the pastor about their family crisis. Well, Mr. Kaldinaldo was no stranger to the pastor since he's well known in the community as a prestigious philanthropist. He approaches the pastor with great honor and asks if he can have just ten minutes of his time because it was an emergency.

Mr. Kaldinaldo approaches and reaches out his hand to Bishop Dagnogfret. He says, "How do you do, sir? I know that you're in a hurry, but I have an emergency of sickness!" "Hello," says Bishop Dagnogfret, "I haven't seen you in a while, but I've heard of the great things you and your family firm continues to do for the community here."

"How may I assist you, sir? What seems to be the urgent matter, my brother? "Well, you see, Bishop, my son Solomon—"

And before he can explain what the matter was, the bishop finished the sentence for him and said, "Solomon, your Solomon, the one that's known for dating multiple women at once has a disease of sickness that he wishes to get prayed for. Huh?"

"Yes! My God, I'm so glad that you're so anointed. When did you find out?"

"Well, he told us earlier today, and we immediately went to the hospital to get blood work. The results are due tomorrow, but we have a deeper issue!" "What's the sickness, first of all?"

"Well, he slept with a female that ended up being a prostitute and HIV positive."

"Really? OMG! Well, we can pray for him. Will he be coming tonight."

"Well, yes, he and his girlfriend are right over there."

"What? Girlfriend?"

"Solomon was committed to one girl," says Mr. Kaldinaldo. "He had changed finally when he met this sweet young lady named Chassaray who's the daughter of Mr. Moolunrig."

"Moolunrig! You mean, as in the Moolunrig Stock Law Firm?"

"Yes."

"My Lord! Does he know about this?"

"No, not yet these two have not even been sexually active yet. They're waiting until marriage."

Bishop Dagnogfret said, "Mr. Kaldinaldo, the other worst part about it is that this girl is a part of the local cult everyone's curious about. She's already started teleporting and drifting into our home after our son. She did it today and he was frantic."

"Whew!!! Lord have mercy. Yes! We have to pray for you all, because this sounds like the work of a witch and mystic powers. Come let's go in and at alter call I want all of you there at once. There will be a special alter call for sicknesses of all sorts as well as general needs. "Is Solomon saved?"

"No, sir!" says Mr. Kaldinaldo.

"Well, I suggest he gets saved tonight."

"Bishop," says Mr. Kaldinaldo, "that's exactly what he's planning on doing tonight."

"Let's go then."

"God bless you! Thank you."

They all enter the sanctuary for praise, and worship had just begun. The family took the front row and began lifting up the Lord Jesus in praise. The conference was full of women in white who were prophets and apostles and elders with white suits and red bowties. There were missionaries standing around with white rags on their heads, holding pails that were filled with warm water and oil, and every five to eight minutes, someone would come before one of the missionaries, bow unto the Lord, and then receive a hot rag dipped in the pail for their face, as cleansing and anointing were indeed taking place. This was indeed a beautiful healing process, and the anointing was flowing very heavy, which meant God was in the place, flowing through all his vessels, and that healing of the Lord was available with the quickness of activated faith. Solomon was looking all around at everyone as if he'd been afraid of what to say to the pastor when, it came to going to the altar. He looked at Chassaray and grabbed her hand and squeezed it and then began to sing along with the praise team. Chassaray looked over at him and saw the tears coming down his face. It broke her heart even more, so she said to Solomon, "The Lord will come through for us no matter what, because he sees your faith."

Solomon says, "I don't know because I'm scared and have doubted so much in the past, when he's lived life as he wanted."

Chassaray says, "You have to forgive me, but I just don't think that he will heal me. Please!"

"Can't you at least just give it a chance? The anointing is so high tonight, and a lot of people are going to receive healing just watch and see."

So, before the last praise song was over, Chassaray begins to lift the Father in heaven with praise and speaking in tongues. Solomon looks over at her, and he began to have hope, although he feared telling the pastor his story on the altar. Solomon's parents grabbed his hand and take him over to the missionaries who were standing around with their hot water and oil pails. They ask that their son be given a rag for his face so that the anointing may penetrate throughout the service. They smiled then reached over to dip a rag for Solomon and told him, "Bless you, my brother."

As they were walking back to their seats, Solomon stopped and began to shiver, as tears were already rolling down his face, he looked at the face of his parents and said, "She's here." They said, "Whom are you speaking of?" Solomon responded with, "The green bow prostitute! Romona!" He says out loud, "She's here because I can feel that same feeling I had when she was connecting with my spirit back at home!"

Mr. and Mrs. Kaldinaldo began to panic, looking around at the pastor for help. They knew the service was about to start. Chassaray rushes over to intercede in prayer to block the connection between him and Romona. As they're huddled in a small circle, a group of disciples, elders, and prophets walked over to the family and asked what was going on. Solomon was standing, there just about to faint. He began telling the saints about this evil female who didn't believe in Jesus and how she had given him a horrible disease and then had the audacity to connect with him in the spirit realm as a witch, after all of the deceit and pain she had already brought to him and his girlfriend Chassaray. Solomon's thinking that maybe she lied about her mom being dead just to get close to him and steal his strength and get him to commit his soul.

Solomon is shaking and saying, "She's here, and she wants to connect with me. OMG! This chick is evil. What am I supposed to do about protection against her after tonight? I'm only a new Christian. She's already threatened to kill my girlfriend if I didn't break up with her."

"What?!" says Chassaray and the elders. "Quick," says the elders. "Let's get him over here back on the altar and pray over him right now instead of waiting for the altar call. This is urgent! Solomon, lay down here on the altar, and said, "We're going to pray over you, okay?"

"Yes," says Solomon. Then he began to shiver and jerk. He said to the disciples, "She's speaking to me, telling me that she's going to block my healing so that I may stay in darkness with her and live in their cult's evil ways." The elders asked him if he'd known that this chick was this evil before he slept with her. He told them about her story of her mom and that she was a very hot-looking chick who seem to have a lot of money. "But it was then I soon realized after our meeting that she must have been involved with the secret cult because of her ex-boyfriend she told me about. Yes, her ex's mom was a deaconess in the church where all these head leaders of that organization serve." "OMG! You're saying that there's a church allowing witches and other leaders to serve—period! Heaven help us. We must pray now, but first, let's alarm all the prophets and elders of what's happening around this church here at the moment." So, they get on the hand-held microphones and give a warning code for everyone to hold their positions in constant prayer language no matter what, until further notice. So now they began praying for Solomon, and about ten minutes into the prayer, the demon girl began to rise up, walking around the church in a circle. The pastor is up at the altar speaking in reference to the anointing and how it works even with the smallest of faith, while at the same time watching the crowd pray over Solomon and wondering what had happened.

Meanwhile, the witch is walking around the church, disturbed because she knows if he's healed and given to Jesus, she can't take him out of the hand of Christ. She wants to have him and have his kids and get rich together, and her plan had worked out perfectly until now.

Romona is very angry! She spots Chassaray and walks up next to her aisle and sits behind her and does a magic trick to make her turn around and look at her face then she says to her, "Will you come with me to the restroom, Chassaray?

I really have an important issue to talk to you about."

Chassaray says, "Excuse me, Romona? What could you possibly want to talk to me about after everything you'd already done you have the audacity to ride your little silly magic carpet to Solomon's house thinking that he would want you! Romona, this is crazy, and it's not of God, now if you're here to praise God, which I don't think you are. It's fine if you're speaking of Jehovah God, but other than that, please do not speak to me. My patience has worn very thin trying to even get my head around the choices that you make to ruin the lives of other people. Romona, you have no conscience about what you do you just do it, and as long as it benefits you, you're okay, but it stops today with Solomon and me. Now please leave us alone and get yourself some Jesus. Solomon doesn't want you, Romona. He was supposed to be my man of God, and you knew it and tried to take him."

Romona interrupts her by saying, "I no longer have Jesus because I gave up when I realized that I wanted him. He's the man I want in this world to reign with."

"Romona, even if you did, neither of you would be a king or queen of any kingdom except the devil's. Your health will fail without Jesus."

"No! See, I know tricks!"

"Tricks," Chassaray says. "Girl, if you don't get your butt up out of this church with that foolishness right now, the Lord is going to deal with you really quick."

Romona's eyes gets really big as she realizes that Chassaary has really had enough of her mess and that she has to do something to make Solomon think of Chassaray as trash, so she defiles her with a magic trick right in the church. She blows in her face and begins to chant, and within seconds, Chasssaray has wart-looking bumps appearing in her face.

Chassaray doesn't even notice them until the next day when she has to go for a play audition. Chassaray sneezes continuously. When she blows and advises her again to please leave and she does. Right after she blows at her face. Chassaray isn't worried because she knows the word of God is sufficient. The bishop is preaching at this time now, and Romona is walking out of the church with a hat and some shades on her face. As soon as she gets near the exit, the bishops calls out hallelujah, then Romona begins to squeal like a cat and shake while running out of the exit The ushers went out behind her in an effort to help, but she had vanished around the corner. At the end of the sermon, the pastor called for anyone needing to come up for prayer for sicknesses of all kinds. Since Solomon was already there, the pastor came over and prayed again, anointing his head with oil, and had him to drink some holy water. After that, Solomon instantly sat up and claimed Jesus as his Lord and savior. He began to confess unto the words of righteousness and believing that Jesus had died and rose on the third day for his sins. Solomon began screaming, "Thank you, Jesus, for my healing!"

Chassaray runs over again and held him in her arms

and cried with him thanking God for his salvation of healing spiritually and physically. The entire family was excited regardless of the doctors' report already taken the day before, which was due tomorrow.

Solomon looked at her with tears in his eyes and pleaded with her, saying, "Chassaray, I love the Lord, for he has truly set me free. I can feel the salvation, Chassaray!" Talking very heavily, he then sighed and began to whisper in her ear. "Chassaray, if it's a miracle, and I'm clean, I promise to God I will do right by you. I'd never hurt you, Chassaray. You're all the girl I've ever wanted. You're beautiful, loving, and smart."

"Solomon, I still love and care for you and want the same things, but let's just take this one step at a time for our hearts' sake. Let's not make any commitments until God says that you're healed. Solomon, I don't mean to be abasing you, but it's a hard decision to make after a devastation like this, but there's one thing for sure here—we both have high hopes and faith. If it so happens that God doesn't turn this thing around, then I will always be your friend because I love you, and I believe that it was God that put us together. It's true, true love sweetie. So for now, let's just remain friends, and we'll stay in prayer about this thing." "Okay, Chassaray, I understand," Solomon says. "Praise the Lord anyway for all things. Amen!"

After the night was over and Solomon returned to his parents' home, he went upstairs to lay down on his bed and thank God for the miracle healing. Solomon had been asleep, but around 2:30 a.m., he awoke and turned on the TV to hear a preacher teaching and prophesying about a man who had just received a miracle healing in the body. Solomon jumped up because he was sure that the pastor was talking about him. He got so excited about taking another test. He wanted to call Chassaray and tell her but fell fast asleep. Solomon calls Chassaray to ask her to meet him at twelve thirty and take off work for the rest of the day and go to the doctor with him to receive his results. Solomon and Chassaray went to the hospital to see the doctor. Mr. Lee comes out, and Solomon says, "I'm hoping for good results, Doc."

Dr. Lee swiftly pulls Solomon into the office, and the door slams and he whips the test out and says, "Solomon, you're positive, and that's not the only thing that's wrong. Solomon, you have high blood pressure, and I must get you on medication for both sicknesses really quick."

Solomon says, "Whoa, whoa, whoa, Doc, not so fast. As far as the HIV testing goes, please allow me to take another test because I received healing last night from the Lord, and he touched my body and I believe that I'm healed."

Dr. Lee looked at Solomon with a confused look and said, "Well, son, I will give you the prescription anyway."

Solomon said, "No, I believe, and with my faith, I already received healing."

Dr. Lee says, "Okay, at your wishes."

Chassaray and Solomon left holding hands and without any medicine prescription. Chassaray called Cream and Regan to meet them at The Wing Café to have afternoon lunch. While they're there sitting, they see some of the gang and cult members come in to get food too. Cream remembers them from the night she and REGAN had the run in. They wondered if the crew had seen them walk into the restaurant, it turns out that they're also accompanied by no one other than Romona herself.

"OMG," says Chassaray. "Those are the guys that use to follow me on the trains, and I'd write down their every move, time and date, and description. That's them—I remember the jackets and faces."

Then CREAM says, "Are you serious! Jesus Christ, those are the same guys who Cream and I had a run in with at the gas station one night. They tried to rob a young lady, and Cream stopped it by interjecting and sending the young lady into the store, and then suddenly the cops pulled up. Lord have mercy. I think we can piece this thing together a little better now."

So Romona obviously has had this entire movement plotted out. She had a plan all along to get to Solomon. She's been following us everywhere. This female really needs help, bad. Let's say something to these people now that we know what their plan is. Cream says, "Who's going to go over and confront them?"

Solomon says, "I will very loudly before his friend, but in the spirit of the Lord, only I shall defend my liberty in order to keep my peace. I will let them know that I'm on to them, and they should stop the madness right now."

So, Solomon went over to the men who were about six in a pack, and Regan went with him.

Solomon says to the men, "Excuse me, my name is Solomon."

The men respond, "Oh yeah, we know who you are," and they began to laugh loudly. Then Romona returns from the restroom.

"Solomon!" she says. "What a surprise. What brings you here?"

"Well, we were already here to have dinner."

Romona says, "Solomon, I want you all to know that I know of your plots to follow me until you got what you wanted, so I've come to let you know that I don't condone your ways of evil and would like to extend an opportunity for you to give your hearts over to the Lord now, because I will not continue to put up with your schemes any period.

The Lord is my witness. If I see that you're following or teleporting to my house, I will call the cops on you immediately."

They were quiet and said nothing in agreement. So, Regan and Solomon walked away with their heads up, and the cult crew just looked at each other and shook their heads, as though they knew something that Solomon and his friend didn't.

Regan says to Solomon, "Can we go and pray right now?" Solomon was shocked but was indeed excited. This gave Solomon that much more courage and faith in Jesus because of what he was seeing in his friend Regan. He knew that the anointing was truly flowing between him and his friends. He was proud to have given his life to Jesus. They went back to the table where the girls were and prayed together for the bond and loving fellowship that they had together. Solomon knew in his heart that soon; his new friend Regan would be giving his heart to the Lord. Solomon told Regan about his experience last night at the altar, of how good it felt to give his heart to Jesus. Solomon told of how he got this instant in love feeling for the Holy Ghost. "Regan man, I know that I'm healed of this disease," says Solomon.

"Yes, Solomon, that's the attitude to have, my brother, and of course, you know that Nicole and I will always be here to support you, no matter what."

"Thank you, Regan, my brother."

It seemed not to be such a big deal that Solomon and

Regan had confronted the cult crew. It was weird because that wasn't the norm for any demon-possessed entity. They're usually causing an uproar in any place. Thanks be to God that He's always in control of all things at all times. Jehovah God is sovereign, and He reigns and none will reign with Him. The word of God says that He will never leave us, nor will he forsake us, even when it seems that things will never get better No matter the level of force of evil. The Bible says that with God, all things are possible, and so Solomon believed and received spiritual healing and salvation. Praise the Lord. In most times in life, we ponder on whether or not we should take that next step, afraid thinking whether if the world has something better to offer. Well, the experience here in reality is just this, that the only land where the grass is ever greener is in the Kingdom's pasture where the true saints of God receive healing. Now this book, you've seen evil at its most disgusting moments, and you've also seen love everlasting even through physical devastation, a parents' love for their child, and most of all, a company and business built off the principles of God.

Stay tuned for the sequel to see where Solomon and Chassaray's relationship is headed after he receives his results after his healing.

Will Solomon lose his job at the stock firm?

Find out just what Romona's plotting and what her next move is. Will she leave the couple alone or disrupt the entire family and everyone connected with it? We all know Romona's destiny, but will she disrupt an entire city to get the man that she wants? IT SEEMS THAT SHE HAS ALWAYS GOTTEN HER WAYS!

This book was documented and written based some events that actually happened in my life, and some where just true scenarios of WHAT COULD HAPPEN IF YOU'RE DISOBEDIENT. These events are shadows of proven entities that follow Christians even today and plagued their lives. Yes! These are demonic spirits that target especially the very elect of God. In times of desperation and pain, we should truly seek deliverance through the HOLY GHOST, which can only be found in Christ. I can truly testify to the fact that Jesus is a deliverer . . .

**MAKE SURE THAT YOU READ THE DISCUSSION IN THE BACK OF THE BOOK TO HELP YOU UNDERSTAND THE REASON FOR THE STORY, BY EXPLAINING WHAT HAS HAPPENED AND, IT WILL ALSO GIVE YOU REFERENCE TO HIS WORD AS WELL. LET ALL OF YOUR FOUNDATION IN LIFE BE BASED OFF OF THE WORD OF GOD NOMATTER HOW SMALL THE TASK, SERVICE, DEED, BUSINESS, REALTIONSHIP MAY BE, WITHOUT THERE BEING A TESTIMONY (EXAMPLE) OF REAL-LIFE ISSUES, WE HAVE NOTHING TO WEIGH THE WORD OF GOD AGAINST. NEVER BE AFRAID TO STAND UP FIRM FOR THE LORD IN FAITH.

GLOSSARY

FOR CHRISTIAN BOOK AND REFERENCING
RE-WRITTEN MANUSCRIPT WITH SMALL GLOSSARY

A GLOSSARY FOR CHRISTIAN UNDERSTANDING

IN SIMPLICITY. The terms may help babes in Christ and even some seasoned Christians understand the subject matter testimony(story) better, even as the characters aren't real. The purpose is to understand the biblical purpose for spiritual growth in Christ's character.

1. ANOINTING ---The power of GOD'S (father) spirit, which empowers saints.

2. TESTIMONY----The testimony is the experience by which we see Christ impacted daily in our lives.

3. NEW TESTIMENT---The NEW testimony, by which CHRIST has been given to us for life, he was NEW TESTIMONY to gentiles. Thus, daily even in our own lives he testifies as NEWNESS OF LIFE, and liberty to be free.

4. HOLY SPIRIT---The SPIRIT OF GOD, by which we move, live, and have our being. It is I AM THE SPIRIT OF GOD living inside those, who excepts Christ as savior, and connects us to HEAVEN.

5. PRINCIPLES--- Principles are the laws of the Bible, by which we shall live and is the basis of righteous living formulated(commanded) for obedience.

6. SYCHRONIZING---When two energies connect for displaying parallel activity.

7. MEMBERS---Members are parts of our spiritual and physical body recognized in a spiritual form unto heaven i.e.. eyes, mind, heart.

8. ALIGNMENT---When is when you conduct your

life(character), your deeds and demeanor unto Christ for death of the physical man, as ye grow in Christ's character.

9. SUBJECT---When we subject our lives unto Christ, which means that we allow our lives to follow the will of GOD.

10. SUBMISSION--- It's when we are under total control of the holy ghost.

11. PALMTREE---A palm tree is the sturdiest trees known near the waters and is deeply rooted. In the Bible it is symbolized as strength.

12. GLORY---The manifestation of who GOD is in the earth.

13. WILL--- Our will (mankind) is in our hearts with our souls and must be aligned with GOD'S will.

14. FAITH---Our faith is our belief in Christ for the unseen manifestations of his glory.

15. MANIFESTATION---Is the product of GOD'S promises, after we've believed.

16. HEART---The heart is a dwelling place for our WILL for either GOD or the enemy.

17. TRIALS---Trial are the situations and issues burdens us, we bare them daily, throughout our Christian walk with long suffering.

18. AGAPE---Is the LOVE that only the holy ghost can give.

19. CULTIVATE---Means to overcome and prosper the good from heaven; to make way sow.

20. SYNONYMOUS--- Means communizing, weigh the difference of a product of a similar interest in

need to be the same.

21. IMPUTE---To have the Lord justify you as he did Abraham as righteous. GOD is the promoter and blesser of our souls.